P9-CEN-366

DATE DUE

Renner Learning Resource Center
Elgin Community College
Elgin, IL 60123

THE
EMPLOYER'S
LEGAL ADVISOR

THE
EMPLOYER'S
LEGAL ADVISOR

- Handling Problem Employees Effectively

- Knowing When and How to
  Work with an Attorney

- Staying Out of Court—or
  Winning Your Case if You Get There

Thomas M. Hanna

AMACOM

American Management Association

New York • Atlanta • Brussels • Chicago • Mexico City • San Francisco
Shanghai • Tokyo • Toronto • Washington, D.C.

Special discounts on bulk quantities of AMACOM books are available to corporations, professional associations, and other organizations. For details, contact Special Sales Department, AMACOM, a division of American Management Association, 1601 Broadway, New York, NY 10019.
Tel: 212-903-8316. Fax: 212-903-8083.
E-mail: specialsls@amanet.org
Website: www. amacombooks.org/go/specialsales
To view all AMACOM titles go to: www.amacombooks.org

This publication is designed to provide accurate and authoritative information in regard to the subject matter covered. It is sold with the understanding that the publisher is not engaged in rendering legal, accounting, or other professional service. If legal advice or other expert assistance is required, the services of a competent professional person should be sought.

Library of Congress Cataloging-in-Publication Data

Hanna, Thomas M.
    The employer's legal advisor : handling problem employees effectively, knowing when and how to work with an attorney, staying out of court—or winning your case if you get there / Thomas M. Hanna.
      p. cm.
    Includes bibliographical references and index.
    ISBN-13: 978-0-8144-0918-3
    ISBN-10: 0-8144-0918-0
    1. Labor laws and legislation—United States—Popular works. I. Title.

KF3455.Z9H365   2007
344.7301—dc22   2006032543

Printing number

10   9   8   7   6   5   4   3   2   1

Contents

Acknowledgments

I would like to express my thanks to my partners in practice, Patricia McFall and Kevin Lorenz, for their assistance. Pat deserves many thanks for her editing advice and assistance and Kevin for his suggestions for Chapter Twelve. Not to be omitted are thanks to my secretary, Susan Berck, for her work on the manuscript. My thanks as well go to Adrienne Hickey, Mike Sivilli, and Louis Greenstein for their hard work and suggestions on making the book readable and informative. I would also like to thank my late partners, V. Lee McMahon and Alan Berger, for bringing me into the practice and for their help and practical advice over the years, and Elmer Davis and Hugh Frank Malone, for whom I worked at the National Labor Relations Board so many years ago and who gave a very young lawyer the kind of leadership he needed. Last but not least, I want to thank Liz for forty-five–plus years of support and encouragement in all endeavors.

THE
EMPLOYER'S
LEGAL ADVISOR

Introduction

In the years following the discovery of the New World, many European nations and eventually the United States issued "letters of marque" to private citizens. A letter of marque authorized a ship's owner to arm his vessel and prey upon the commerce of a warring nation, keeping whatever booty he "liberated" at cannon point for his own profit (minus a share for his government, of course). These vessels and their crews were known as *privateers* or *corsairs*, and without a letter of marque, the commander and crew of such a ship would have been nothing less than pirates. Article I, Section 8 of the U.S. Constitution authorizes Congress to grant "letters of marque and reprisal." In fact, Congress did issue such letters against the Barbary Pirates in 1800 and during the War of 1812.

The contemporary version of privateers is much more sophisticated. They are known today as "private attorney generals" and are authorized by law to collect a fee from alleged violators of specific laws, especially employment discrimination laws. The federal government, as well as many state governments, has enabled private citizens to sue for alleged violations of civil and employment rights and to recover back pay, front pay, emotional distress damages, and punitive damages for such claimed losses and injuries. These lawsuits are almost entirely filed in federal or state courts, where a jury decides guilt or innocence as well as the amount of any damages to be awarded.

There may be some legislative limits imposed on some types of damage, but the legislation also usually provides for the award of attorneys' fees. In such cases, the plaintiff's attorney assumes, by his own initiative, the mantle of private attorney general and seeks to earn his fee at the expense of some hapless employer either by means of litigation that is successful in some degree or by settlement of the claim. By the time the employer pays the company attorney, the plaintiff's attorney, and the damages awarded in one of these cases, the company has lost many dollars, and much productivity is required to offset these costs.

The Costs of Litigation

Actual awards and attorney fee expenses in the private sector have not been comprehensively documented, to my knowledge. However, one website (HR AnswerLink, November 19, 2005) claimed that average litigation costs were $50,000 per case and that average settlements were $200,000. That cost estimate appears to be too low if one is thinking of a hotly contested federal trial that goes to a jury (although it might represent costs up to some point of settlement short of trial). Meanwhile, the settlement average of $200,000 may be too high, at least in the Midwest and mid-South where I have most of my experience.

Reliable figures are available from the U.S. Equal Employment Opportunity Commission (EEOC) at its website (www.eeoc.gov/ stats). In 2005, more than 75,000 charges of employment discrimination were filed with the EEOC; in addition, 417 suits were filed in federal court that year. The EEOC reported that in 2005, $107.7 million in monetary benefits was recovered, compared with $168.1 million in 2004. EEOC filings and lawsuits are but the tip of the iceberg: When you consider the foregoing statistics, remember that most cases of employment discrimination are not filed by the EEOC but by the so-called private attorney generals! Most discrimination cases take from two to three years to resolve. Between 2003 and 2005, 235,973 charges were filed with the EEOC and only 1,200 were the subject of an EEOC suit. If only 20 percent of the remaining charges resulted in private civil actions, that means that there were almost 47,000 real or threatened civil actions during those three years, generating huge costs and defense efforts.

The Employer's Need to Act

When I worked for the National Labor Relations Board (NLRB) in the early 1960s, I found that most employers had minimal if any documentation to support the discharges of errant employees. As the years progressed and litigation increased, employers became aware of the need for greater effort to support decision making that affected employees. Those employer efforts substantially increased with the advent of civil rights litigation. While for the most part the majority of my clients did a good job dealing with their employees, someone would invariably try to exploit any honest mistake they made. My clients often found (and still find) that plaintiffs' lawyers try to find any questionable act or omission and then exploit it for their clients' purposes. They will do anything they can to make the employer seem incompetent, callous, reckless, and discriminatory to support their claim of discrimination.

It occurred to me that owners and managers of businesses could benefit from advice on how to deal with difficult employee problems and related issues, including advice on what pitfalls to avoid. This is true of companies that are large enough to be subject to state or federal jurisdiction in employment law cases as well as businesses that have geographically separated small operations. Even human resources professionals in large businesses may confront problems that are new to them and may have no ready resource for advice unless they have access to an experienced attorney.

This book serves as a ready reference for both the executive suite and freestanding operations. The advice contained here applies to any kind of anticipated discipline or action that has an adverse effect on an employee, especially one in a legally protected classification. The purpose of this book is to assist individual entrepreneurs, managers who lack immediately accessible or affordable professional assistance, and human resources professionals in taking action to avoid or minimize litigation that may result from claims of employment discrimination before a state or federal court, a state or federal administrative agency, or a labor arbitrator. In short, this book teaches them how to apply "street smarts" in employee matters. A secondary purpose is to provide guidance and insight into employment problems that may result in litigation.

I began my career working as an attorney for the Fort Worth, Texas, regional office of the NLRB. In those days, a person, union, or employer who believed that there had been a violation of the National Labor Relations Act filed a charge with the NLRB and presented evidence supporting that charge. The board agent assigned to the case would contact the other party for any defense it might choose to assert. In the event the regional office believed that violation of the law had occurred, a complaint would be issued, and the matter would be heard by an administrative law judge. Some of the judges were perfect, some were perfectly awful, and some were average. Most of the time, the judges were pretty good at resolving issues regarding who was telling the truth and who was not, and they usually gave factually detailed reasons for their decisions.

If a witness was not believed regarding a given fact or issue, the losing side, at least, had an explanation from the judge (which is more than litigants in a court of law ever get from a jury). A losing party could appeal both the factual and legal conclusions to the NLRB itself. The administrative law judge's credibility decisions were usually not subject to review upon appeal, but neither are a jury's credibility decisions. Monetary awards under the National Labor Relations Act were confined to back pay. The NLRB was and is a highly political body because its members are appointed by the President of the United States, and it is usually composed of two members from the minority party and three from the majority party. Nevertheless, the NLRB was charged with enforcing a law enacted by the Congress and it did its institutional best, subject to the political leanings of its members. While the system was far from perfect it did have administrative controls built into the system that prevented an explosion of willy-nilly, unmeritorious litigation. Today's civil rights legislation has vested control in the court system with the result that questionable claims have little chance of being weeded out with finality, let alone by the government at its expense. Instead the employer must engage an attorney and spend time, money, and energy to persuade a court or jury that the case should be dismissed.

When Congress enacted today's employment and civil rights legislation; it did not attempt to duplicate the system established by the National Labor Relations Act. At first, only federal judges could decide alleged violations of Title VII of the Civil Rights Act, and they could award equitable relief only in the form of injunctions and similar court orders for equitable relief, back pay, front pay, and reinstatement as well as attorneys' fees. Later legislation provided for jury trials and added the right to recover so-called "actual" damages as well as punitive damages.

As new laws—such as the Age Discrimination in Employment Act (ADEA) and Americans with Disabilities Act (ADA)—were enacted, the remedial provisions under Title VII were incorporated into those laws. The loss of experienced judges as fact finders and their replacement by juries has created greater uncertainty about the outcome of any given piece of litigation.

Why this uncertainty? It is because a plaintiff's attorney will do everything in her power to remove potential jurors she considers "too smart" or "too sophisticated" to believe her client's claims of discrimination and damage. In a trial, attorneys have "preemptory strikes," which allow them to remove a potential juror from the jury panel without any justification whatsoever. The most likely objects of a plaintiff's attorney's preemptory strikes are managers, professionals of every kind, and other persons who evince a no-nonsense attitude because they understand the difficulties a problem employee may create.

In addition, these desirable jurors invariably try to get out of jury service in the first place because they have a busy lifestyle and can little afford to sit on a case that may take one to three weeks or even longer to hear. The people who can devote this time and who often compose the jury are much more inclined to be in sympathy with the worker. Potential jurors most likely consist of hourly workers whose employer is willing to supplement their jury pay, unemployed people, homemakers, and retired people (but not retired professionals and managers who will be challenged for the same reasons as persons active in the profession). Sheltered from the realities of management and supervision, conditioned by television and media "sob stories" and reports of large verdicts, these folks often tend to be sympathetic to the employee. Besides, who has not known someone in their fifties who was laid off work after years of service? Who has not seen someone treated unfairly by a callous boss or employer? Because juries are attuned to the idea of "fairness" rather than the complexities of business or industrial life, or the law as instructed by the court, employers have greater need now more than ever before to prove their employment decisions were fair and reasonable as well as nondiscriminatory.

Sooner or later, nearly every employer will be subject to a claim that it violated one employment law or another. The reason for this is simple: Employees who have been fired are angry and will strike back at the employer if they can find the means to do so. The public is conditioned to think in terms of discrimination, and if individuals perceive that they are protected by a law, it costs nothing to file a discrimination charge with a state or federal agency. The problem arises when an individual (or class action) claim matures into a civil action in state or federal court.

This book is designed to aid entrepreneurs, managers, supervisors, and human resources professionals in their efforts to protect their company by avoiding costly mistakes, establishing a protective barrier around each decision that may result in litigation, and preparing to deal with any future charge or civil action. Nothing can ensure you of absolute protection from unscrupulous lawyers or government blundering, but if you are the master of the facts and preserve those facts, you will be well served by your diligence.

CHAPTER  ONE

Employment Law at Work

This book is not *My Life in Court* (although there is some of that by necessity), nor is it an explanation of the nuances of employment law.* There is no shortage of written material giving general advice on all of the federal laws prohibiting discrimination and harassment at work, but knowing the letter of the law will not necessarily assist you in dealing with the employment problems you may face in real life.

Few of us face a crisis every day or week, but it takes only one event to generate a civil action that could cost you hundreds of thousands if not millions of dollars to defend. Perhaps more to the point, you—as a decision maker or key advisor—may become a star witness for your company's defense. Thus, before the trial, you will be a key resource who must answer numerous interrogatory questions, dig up hundreds or thousands of documents, assist company attorneys in taking depositions, and, without doubt, give a lengthy deposition of your own.

---

*A brief description of key employee laws can be found at the end of this book.

The Burden on the Employer

Unfortunately, it's not enough in our day and age simply to make sure that no disparate treatment occurred, no harassment took place, or no company policy was violated. There is a much greater burden placed on the employer.

For example, one approach that plaintiffs' lawyers use to get a case before a jury is a claim of "pretext." To make this claim, they must show that the reason given for an employer's action is not the actual or true reason, which gives the employee the opportunity to claim that the actual reason for the action was discriminatory. The employee has the burden of persuading the jury that the employer's motives were discriminatory. However, this burden may be satisfied by mere argument (as opposed to actual evidence). The employer caught in this predicament still has the opportunity to show that his motives were not discriminatory, but that's a heavy burden. You do not want to be in the awkward position of having to explain to a court the discrepancy between the real reason you fired someone and the reason you gave her. The real burden comes much earlier, in making sure you know what you are doing when discharging someone.

Things an Employer Must Do

Often an employer wishes to discharge an employee based on subjective factors, such as bad feelings or instinct, rather than on demonstrable facts. However well founded that opinion may be, it will not suffice to form a strong defense if the employee is in a legally protected category based on race, sex, color, religion, age, or disability (just to name a few). Therefore, the employer must:

- Be alert for problems and keep good documentation of all employment actions.

- Investigate complaints promptly and professionally.

- Preserve evidence.

- Reach a reasoned decision based on objective facts that can be proven in a court of law.

Employers must know how to manage these steps. They must be able to identify potential problems before they get out of hand. Where problems have arisen, they must be able to make it apparent to any state or federal agency or plaintiff's lawyer that the disgruntled employee's claim of discrimination is flawed and without merit.

The primary tool to achieve this result is the accumulation and preservation of evidence necessary for defending any employment decision that may be questioned (or, in the context of a union contract, any decision that may lead to a grievance and arbitration). Competently preserving the facts underlying an employment decision and putting those facts together in a persuasive manner prepares you to prove to any judge or jury that you (or your organization) acted reasonably and fairly. The principles in play here apply with equal vigor to any employment situation that is likely to lead to employee discipline, discharge, or demotion. Many of these principles are also of value in guiding you as you deal with nondisciplinary issues such as hiring.

The Realities of Employment Cases

In the ideal world, an offended employee would consult a knowledgeable attorney who would tell her to forget about suing her former employer because her case is without legal or factual merit. You cannot count on that happening in the real world. It is much more likely that the attorney will examine the claim in an effort to find enough legitimacy to file a superficially credible lawsuit designed to extract, at the very least, a nuisance-value settlement from your company.

One of the reasons employment issues stir up so much litigation is the fact that with most state and federal offenses, attorneys' fees are determined by the court and awarded to the "prevailing party" (that is, the party that wins the case). If you are an employer, you can forget about being a prevailing party because the standards for awarding attorney fees to an employer are impossibly high. On the other hand, if you are an employee-plaintiff, the standards are laughably low. An employee-plaintiff can file a lawsuit with many allegations, lose all but one claim, and still proclaim prevailing party status. (In law school, we were taught that when courts engage in the process of legal reasoning, they sometimes assume that something is true even though it may not be true. This is known as a "legal fiction." The manner in which prevailing party status is now determined is just such a legal fiction. Until either the case law or the statute law changes, the employer will remain a target for plaintiff's lawyers. You must do everything possible to avoid being an "easy target.")

In a recent case I tried, an employee who had been discharged for misconduct sued his former employer in a five-count complaint. The federal court dismissed four of the counts, including the employee's most important claim. During the trial, the jury awarded the defendant damages of $5,500, a sum so low that it was extremely unlikely to result in an appeal. The judge then proceeded to give the plaintiff's attorneys fees and expenses of approximately $123,000—nearly twenty-five times greater than the damages given by the jury.

If It Can Be Filed, It Will Be Filed

I take no pleasure in saying this about my profession, but the fact is that attorneys often have a greater financial interest in the outcome of litigation than does the plaintiff. This was a breach of an attorney's ethical duties in times past, but today such standards no longer exist. In fact, attorneys—sometimes often finance litigation out of their own pocket. It is no wonder, then, that employment litigation is one of the more fertile fields available to attorneys today. It is possible that with the advent of promised reforms affecting cases of medical malpractice, asbestos and silicosis claims, and the increased standards of proof product liability cases, those particular civil actions will diminish in both volume and value to plaintiffs' attorneys.*

As those easy targets disappear, plaintiffs' lawyers will be casting about for new ones, which might include you or your company. Generally, any civil action that can be filed will be filed. Some unscrupulous attorneys will bring an action they know is without merit simply in the hopes of coercing a settlement from the hapless employer. There's a significant settlement value in almost every lawsuit because employment law cases are factually intensive and are often filed in federal court, where attorneys put in hundreds of hours—at very expensive hourly rates merely in discovery and pretrial procedures alone. State court litigation may be equally complex and is seldom accompanied by attorney fees at bargain rates. In addition to the possibility of an attorney who may milk an issue for the sake of a fee, there is also the constant risk of the offended employee consulting an attorney who is trying to make his mark in the world and who attacks your company with unusual vigor. That alone may run up the company's legal bills to an intolerable level.

---

*Plaintiff's Lawsuits Against Companies Sharply Decline, *Wall Street Journal*, August 26, 2006.

If you are the master of the facts and can demonstrate that actions you took against an employee were fair and reasonable, you have gone a long way toward winning your case or bringing about a settlement on less than ruinous terms. Further, you will have the satisfaction of knowing you did all that could be reasonably expected under the circumstances.

Discrimination Cases

Direct proof of a discriminatory intent on the part of the employer is unusual. Direct proof most often takes the form of verbal or written remarks that indicate a discriminatory motive on the part of the person making the comments. Instead, most discrimination claims are based on circumstantial evidence. The great preponderance of these claims fall under either the "disparate treatment" model or the "adverse impact" model.

In a "disparate treatment" claim the plaintiff complains that her treatment by the employer was different from that of "similarly situated" employees because of her status as a member of a protected class (age, race, sex, disability, etc.). There is another form of "disparate treatment" claim in which the employee asserts that his treatment was discriminatory because the employers reasons for acting were false and nothing more than a "pretext" for taking action and the real reason was an intent to discriminate. There may be allegations relating to both theories in a "disparate treatment" claim.

In an "adverse impact" claim, it is some policy or practice of the employer that a court of law determines to be legally unjustified or unnecessary so as to disproportionately affect a protected class thereby discriminating unlawfully against those persons.

During an employment discrimination trial involving disparate treatment cases, there is a three-step dance that takes place in federal court and some state courts. The first step is the plaintiff's proof of a "prima facie" case: that he was in a protected classification, that the job was one for which he was qualified (or performing satisfactorily), that another employee (of another race, sex, etc.) was treated more leniently or given a preference. Alternatively the plaintiff attacks the employer's reason for acting as untrue or exaggerated and merely a "pretext" for discrimination.

The second step is for the employer to show either that there were no similarly situated employees or that the employee was not treated differently or, if the claim is "pretext," that its actions were for legitimate, nondiscriminatory reasons.

At that point the third step begins: The employee-plaintiff must refute the employer's evidence. In the context of a "pretext" case this involves showing that the employer's articulated reasons were but a pretext for discrimination. The usual means for this is a claim that some or all of the facts on which the employer relied were untrue, or exaggerated or somehow disproportionate to the reasons for the employer's decision. This does not mean that the plaintiff must totally discredit the employer's reason for acting; he must only cast enough doubt to raise a factual issue as to whether or not what the defense asserted was the true reason for the employer's action.

If the court or jury decides that the defense is not true, or not the real reason, the fact finder then has the task of weighing the employer's motives and thus have the opportunity to infer that unlawful discrimination was the real reason for the action. That factual issue is usually decided by a jury, unless a jury is waived or you are before an administrative body established under state law. If the plaintiff can clear this hurdle, he can argue to a jury that the employer's real reason must have been intentional discrimination. The jury must then determine whether or not the employer intentionally discriminated against the employee. If there has been a strong showing of "pretext," the employer's fate is in the hands of a jury or whomever is charged with fact finding.

Defending Your Company

How often have we heard "The best defense is a good offense"? Applying that principle here, the idea is for you to make as solid a case as is possible by preserving evidence showing the employee's errors, misconduct, or other deficiency. That evidence will show that you exercised good judgment in decision making as well as demonstrating that you had a nondiscriminatory reason for taking action, thus providing a barrier to the employee proving any form of "disparate treatment." The prudent employer will also act on that information in a manner that will convey to any potential fact-finder (such as a judge or jury) that its actions were fair and reasonable under the circumstances.

During the process, the employer must also make an effort to convey its judgment and actual reasons for its decision to the employee at the time action is taken, all in an effort to show that the reason for action was "bona fide" and not pretextual. If you clearly prove that the employee engaged in unacceptable conduct and you consistently administered discipline, you should win the case. (This assumes that the employer and its managers and supervisors have not provided direct evidence of discriminatory intent by inappropriate verbal or written comments.)

Once an employee who has been confronted squarely with the employer's decision and the reasons for that decision opts to file a charge or consult an attorney, he must relay what his employer has given as the reason for discipline (demotion, non-promotion, etc.) or risk loss of credibility when that reason is put forth by the company's defense. This is especially true if the reasons were given to the employee in writing in the same verbiage that would appear in any termination slip placed in the personnel file. If the decision was clear, unequivocal, and in keeping with the facts uncovered by the investigation, the employee cannot easily conceal what he has been told orally or in writing as the reason for his discipline or discharge when taking his case before a private attorney, the U.S. Equal Employment Opportunity Commission, or the National Labor Relations Board. The employee is then compelled to deal with your defense by showing it to be untrue or more severe than actions taken with respect to other employees who are not in one of the protected classifications.

The important point here is that by giving the employee the real and unequivocal reason for your actions when those reasons are supported by hard evidence, you have taken the first step in erecting a legal barrier to protect your company.* In the absence of direct evidence of discrimination, this means that those attorneys or agencies suing an employer must search to see if the employer's actions were pretextual or not in conformity with similar previous decisions—in other words, designed to cover up the fact that the real intent was discriminatory. A prosecutor will be less inclined to take action when there appears to be a valid reason for discipline because the possibility of unlawful discrimination is not readily apparent and because a subsequent legal action would be a waste of time and resources.

When an employee acts as her own attorney, thorough documentation is invaluable in achieving a prompt dismissal of the claim.

---

*It is not necessary to disclose all of the evidence to the employee at the time you take action, especially if you wish to protect the identity of witnesses. The ultimate reason itself is sufficient to put the employee on notice. Please note that some states have laws that require an employer to permit employees to review their personnel records under certain circumstances and in that event you should not conceal any facts from the employee because it may preclude their subsequent use in litigation.

Self-representation is known as *pro se* (for oneself) representation. Federal employment discrimination laws usually permit an employee who can't afford or find an attorney to appear *pro se*, and blank pleading forms are provided to the employee for this purpose. If you receive such a form filled out by a former employee (or a disgruntled current one), take it seriously and send it to your attorney at once.

The employee herself is seldom in a position to dispute all of the facts a complete investigation has discovered. Because she must admit that she was told the reason for the employer's actions, she has undermined her own claim to the extent that she has demonstrated that there *may* be a nondiscriminatory reason for the employer's action. To overcome this, the employee must then attempt to work around the employer's reasons for action by providing an acceptable explanation of how she was victimized. If any attorney or agency finds an obvious flaw in the employee's claim, it may end the possibility of the lawsuit.

Even if a civil action follows, the actions taken by the employer for good cause and the employer's straight-to-the-point, relevant decision making will enhance the defense because it will be more difficult for the plaintiff-employee to prove pretext or other error. It will also reduce defense attorney fees and help prove to a judge and jury that the actions taken were fair and reasonable. It is far better that fact finding in court or before an administrative body focus on well-defined, relevant facts rather than a haphazard defense based upon after-the-fact defenses or poorly understood information.

Always remember that when a company is sued, it may have one or more employees or former employees working against it, sometimes in their own self-interest and sometimes out of a vindictive spirit. This possibility underscores the need for competent and timely action on the part of an employer.

Competent fact preservation, clear decision making, and good communication are the essential ingredients to a successful defense of any employment law claim. Make no mistake: Even the best judges will be intolerant of an employer who does not keep good records and take elementary steps to justify its actions. The same ingredients—careful preservation of facts, clear decision making, and conscientious communication—will also help you when faced with a jury. Despite court instructions telling them that they are to consider only whether or not your actions were discriminatory as a matter of law, juries invariably question your actions to see if they are fair and reasonable. Even worse, juries may second-guess your decision based on their limited knowledge of business and industry practice or what they think "should have been done." If you do your job correctly, though, you may have the jury thinking instead, "They should have fired her long before this."

Employer's Legal Pad—Chapter One Checklist

No one wants to get sued by a disgruntled current or former employee. No one enjoys the demand on their time, the strain on the company, the financial burden, and the enormous distraction. Yet sometimes litigation happens, and since you don't know when it will happen, here are three important action items for all employers all the time:

1. Document every employment decision, including decisions to hire, not hire, discipline, promote, and demote.

2. Communicate the true and actual business-related reason for every employment decision you make.

3. Look into all complaints promptly, and maintain records of your investigations.

CHAPTER TWO

Good Intentions Are Only a Start

If you manage people long enough, you will eventually have to fire, demote, or discipline an employee (in the field of human resources and employment law, this is known as taking an "adverse action"). In my experience, a discrimination lawsuit tends to occur when an employee (or, more likely, his attorney) does not believe that the employer has the facts to support the adverse action it took against the employee.

It has been my experience that the great majority of employers have no desire to discriminate unlawfully against anyone. To be sure, there are personal bias issues, but these do not necessarily involve a deliberate intention to discriminate.

A Shock to the Client

Bias usually takes the form of sweeping assumptions that cannot be shown to be justified by the evidence. Years ago, I represented a client with a small manufacturing plant that had certain jobs it assigned to men and other, lower-paid, jobs that it assigned to women. The men's jobs were hot, heavy, and dirty and required a degree of mechanical skill. The women's jobs were clean and light, mostly performed while seated, and required finger dexterity. This allocation of work was consistent with thinking that prevailed at the time and through much of the industrial revolution. In fact, one of the appellate judges who heard the case commented that women had greater finger dexterity than men and would probably prefer "clean" jobs. This comment was much to the chagrin of the EEOC's attorney, who considered such remarks sexist but could say nothing for fear of offending the judge.

It was a shock to the client when the company was sued for sex discrimination (of which they were clearly guilty) under Title VII of the Civil Rights Act. There was no evil intent present. (In fact, the owner and manager was a woman who had inherited the plant from her late husband.) It was simply a failure to recognize the sweeping nature of workplace change brought about by Title VII and case law developments resulting from widespread litigation.

Fortunately for the client, there were no serious damages in the form of back pay because during litigation, all of the company's jobs were opened to women and it was literally years before anyone accepted what had once been a male-only job. Nevertheless, there was a lawsuit based on a bias that had developed from what had been the industrial practice in past years.* In addition, the client was saddled with fees from the plaintiff's attorney by reason of the "prevailing party" rule.

---

*In past years, numerous laws were enacted to protect women from certain work deemed harmful to their health. I venture no opinion as to the merit or lack of merit of those protective statutes, which are now outdated by rule of law, but predict that they someday may reappear in somewhat different form.

Shielding Yourself from Charges of Discrimination

While an employer may lack an actual intent to discriminate, policies and practices that cannot be clearly related to "business necessity" may be alleged to have a disparate impact that has a discriminatory effect upon persons in a protected category. The disparate impact doctrine implies that unlawful discrimination took place because a particular rule or practice disproportionately affects persons in a protected class and cannot be justified by a reasonable, nondiscriminatory factor. The case just cited represents a perfect example of the disparate impact a rule or policy may have. Another example has been the requirement of a high school diploma when it could not be shown to be necessary (being desirable does not count). Almost every employee or applicant is in a protected category except able-bodied Caucasian, Christian, heterosexual males, born in the United States, and under age 40—and even they may be entitled to some measure of protection if they are in a union-organized bargaining unit, have veteran's reemployment rights, or can claim reverse discrimination.

Despite the absence of bad intentions, circumstances giving rise to employment discrimination lawsuits have a way of sneaking up on the unwary and unprepared. For example, Shari, a recent divorcee, often teased supervisors with sexual innuendo and photos of herself in risqué lingerie and by flaunting her sexual activities, some of which purportedly took place on company premises. No one in authority had the gumption to put a halt to Shari's conduct. It was only after she was fired for excess absenteeism that she claimed she'd been the victim of sexual discrimination because she would not date Sam, an unmarried supervisor. I won't bore you with the details of how we got out of the case without loss, but I will say that potentially serious litigation might have been avoided if Shari's employer had taken prompt action to stop her sexually suggestive conduct and outright provocations as well as discouraging male management from responding in a positive manner.

What often seems to be a routine discharge for obvious misconduct can become a nightmare of litigation taking years to resolve. You may not know about all the events that have occurred between employees or between an employee and a supervisor until after charges are filed or litigation begins. Remarks that are meant to be funny may be seen by some as offensive, and they may then be used against the company even if the employee was not truly offended at the time of utterance. After a discharge the ex-employee may find it opportune to claim the remarks offensive. Even employees who were not directly involved with the remark may find it convenient to claim offense if they can utilize the remark by claiming it had an effect on them, for example, a racial slur. How many times have off-color remarks passed between men and women, only to be ignored, until someone is denied a promotion or fired?

That's why it is practically impossible to shield yourself from allegations of discrimination, harassment, disparate treatment, etc.—and why every employer should be prepared.

Constructive Discharge and Other Claims

I remember one case in which employees in a rural area had seen too many African-American comics on cable TV using the "N" word. In a misplaced effort at camaraderie with Charles, an African-American employee, Gene, a white fellow worker, repeated one of those offensive jokes while on a fishing trip. (The trip was strictly among employees and had nothing to do with the employer.) At some later point, Charles became angry with the company for reasons having nothing to do with race (he was made to pay for equipment he damaged). He quit and filed a lawsuit claiming he'd been "constructively discharged." Constructive discharge is a legal theory used by plaintiffs who quit their employment allegedly because working conditions were such that no reasonable person could be expected to continue in employment.

Charles claimed that remarks constituting racial harassment caused him to quit (after he had secured another job). During the trial, Charles cited the use of the "N" word as part of his justification for quitting. Despite the company's best efforts to explain what had really happened, the innocent if misguided use of the unsavory word caused a real problem in litigation.

Many employees just do not know how to conduct themselves and thus are in need of guidance. We may all easily make a careless remark that can be misunderstood or taken with exaggerated significance by a listener. Only recently, a prominent television personality settled a sexual harassment suit based on intemperate remarks he purportedly made to a female subordinate. Such events happen every day. What is funny or acceptable to one employee may seriously offend another. Something that was either not offensive or only moderately offensive at the time it was said or done has a way of becoming an issue in subsequent litigation when the employment relationship turns sour.

While it is true that the harassment must be severe or prolonged before it becomes actionable in a court of law, there is no justification for permitting such behavior to go on, let alone reaching the stage where liability is created. Sterilizing the workplace is no fun and probably uncalled for but, for better or worse, the "good old boy" attitudes and mannerisms of yesteryear do not easily coexist with today's employment laws.

Here are just a few of the more prominent claims that may be alleged against an employer or manager in state or federal court or before some administrative agency:

- Discrimination and harassment based on race, color, or national origin.

- Sexual discrimination and harassment.

- Age discrimination.

- Religious discrimination and harassment.

- Discrimination related to pregnancy.

- Disability discrimination, including failure to provide reasonable accommodation.

- Family Medical Leave Act (FMLA) discrimination.

- Discrimination against union or "concerted" activities.

- Retaliation for wage/hour and overtime claims.

- Disciplinary problems under a union contract.

- Disciplinary problems when the employee is a current or recent workers compensation claimant.

- Retaliation for having filed charges alleging any of the foregoing.

- Discrimination against whistle-blowers (people who complain or report their employer for violations or alleged violations of state or federal law).

- Individual state employment laws may provide protection in certain respects that differs from federal law, for example, sexual preference.

- Discrimination by reason of filing Occupational Safety and Health Act (OSHA), Mine Safety and Health Act (MSHA), and related complaints.

- Discrimination against veterans.

Please note that several diverse allegations may be included in a single action and it becomes the employer's burden to defend each claim on the facts.

Because it is not always possible to know everything that is going on at your company or workplace, there must be a routine procedure developed to help you ferret out problems before they develop and to prevent making mistakes in decision making. To avoid or minimize liability, there are five fundamental actions that need to be taken:

1. To the best of your ability, know what is going on at the business.

2. Document events concerning discipline and performance, especially those that may involve a discrimination claim.

3. Review the facts and your operations to see if there is any possibility of overt or inadvertent discrimination by reason of policy or practice.

4. Take appropriate action in a fair and reasonable manner.

5. Take that action in a way that demonstrates fairness and reasonableness to outsiders.

I cannot overemphasize this last element. No matter how "right" you may be, there is always someone who will take issue with your judgment and try to nitpick the decision. The employer must be in a position to convince most outsiders that it acted fairly and reasonably under the circumstances.

Employer's Legal Pad—Chapter Two Checklist

Before you consider an adverse action, make sure you've got your employment-law ducks in a row.

- Review company policies. Are they up to date? Do they comply with all local, state, and federal regulations?

- Be prepared to explain to an outsider who is not familiar with your business or industry why your decision was reasonable.

Consider offering antidiscrimination and sexual harassment workshops to managers and supervisors. Some people don't know how to conduct themselves in the workplace, what's funny (and what isn't), and what language is appropriate. It's part of your job to make sure they know what is acceptable and what is not.

CHAPTER THREE

Eliminating Problems Before They Arise

There are many things you can do to eliminate problems in the workplace before they arise. Taking such steps can help you avoid costly lawsuits and legal problems.

Prompt Correction of Employees

When disciplining employees, taking prompt corrective action is key. The offending employee must be called to account for her misconduct in a timely and reasonable fashion. In the event of performance errors, you must be able to prove that you tried to work with the employee to improve her performance. Juries always respect the fact that you gave the employee a second chance or tried to assist her in learning how to perform her job.

As I write this, I am dealing with a case where a store employee was guilty of excess absenteeism during his probationary period. Prompt disciplinary action was not taken for two reasons: The store manager was lenient on the first offense, and on later offenses, the manager was away from the store so often that he never got around to confronting the employee until after the employee had sustained an on-the-job injury. By that time, the store manager was fed up and fired the employee. The employee's excuse was that he had taken off work to consult an attorney about a workers compensation claim. The resulting dismissal generated a workers compensation retaliation claim in a state court civil action because the employee's lawyer claimed that the attorney consultation constituted protected activity under state law. The problem most likely could have been avoided if the employer had disciplined the employee on his first or second absenteeism offense.

Employee Reviews of the Company

Especially in the context of a nonunion operation, it is a good idea once a year to require each employee to complete a review of the company. Each employee should complete, sign, and date a form that asks questions like the following:

- What do you like about your job?

- What do you dislike about your job?

- Has your supervisor provided you with the necessary assistance to do your job properly? If not, please explain.

- Do you get along with your coworkers and do they get along with you? If not, please explain.

- Has any supervisor or coworker discriminated against you? If so, please explain.

- Has any supervisor or coworker harassed or intimidated you? If so, please explain.

- Has the company or your supervisor treated you unfairly? If so, please explain.

- Are there any company policies that you dislike? If so, please explain.

- Are you aware that if you have a complaint about discriminatory treatment or harassment of any kind, affecting yourself or others, you should promptly advise _____ [insert name of contact] about what has happened?

- If you would like to make additional comments, please do so below.

Most discrimination charges must be filed within a period ranging from six months to three hundred days of the discriminatory event. However, if the court finds that an alleged "continuing" violation exists, the claim could reach back for a period of years. This means that evidence of harassment or unlawful discriminatory intention that might otherwise be stale is revitalized, given life, and used against the employer.

What happens if an employee makes a complaint about discriminatory conduct that has been ongoing for a period of years and is therefore continuing in nature, but the so-called problems have not been mentioned in any reviews she made of the company? Her credibility will be severely impaired because her claim is inconsistent with her written statements.

An annual review such as that proposed above will also let you know about nagging minor violations that could mature into a serious case. They will also enable an employer to nip an obvious problem in the bud.

Note that one of the items in the employee review establishes a contact person for purposes of reporting alleged discrimination or harassment. This contact should be someone who is far enough up the chain of command so that she will not be the person accused of misconduct or his pal. Sometimes it is preferable to name more than one person as a contact because of problems with availability, possible friendship with an alleged offender, and in the case of sexual harassment it may be preferable to report offensive conduct to a member of the same sex.

Negative answers on the employee review give you notice that a follow-up investigation is needed. Go to the employee and make certain you have his entire story (which he has hopefully written in detail), and then investigate to determine the truth of the matter. Sort out the facts and reply to the employee. If corrective action is needed, take it. If the employee was wrong or has overstated the problem, review the issue with him and put your response in writing and keep it on file with the review.

If the employee makes only positive or neutral responses to the review, the result is that "his lips are sealed" by his own words and his failure to report previous allegations of discrimination. By way of example suppose an employee claims harassment over a period of years that was so extreme she felt the need to quit and sue, claiming that she was constructively discharged. If you can reach into her personnel file and show that for all of the previous years she never once complained of harassment or of other problems, nor did she notify anyone that she was being harassed, her credibility will be severely impaired and her inaction may be fatal to the claim. This example will hold true regardless of the nature of the discrimination claimed.

The responses you make to the form and your investigation go a long way in minimizing any liability you might have. Usually, employers receive positive answers from their employees on such forms. If an employee subsequently charges the company with discrimination after he has written a positive review, he can be confronted with answers that are inconsistent with his charge and asked to explain all inconsistencies. This is especially true if the employee tries to dredge up some past event that he now says was objectionable but which he never reported to management. He cannot now claim that he did not have a good opportunity to do so since he had an opportunity to write a review of the company's performance. If something has occurred between reviews, the employee will have had the opportunity to notify the necessary contact person.

By requiring employees to complete, in writing, an annual review of important employment issues within the company, the employer ferrets out problems before they become so great that resolution is difficult. Prompt action designed to resolve complaints that have merit helps you not only to be reasonable but to appear reasonable when your actions are questioned by outsiders. Never underestimate the value of appearing fair, consistent, and reasonable. If you are ever rigorously cross-examined, you will be glad you took a careful, prudent approach when dealing with employee complaints and this holds true for problem employees as well. If the complaints are without factual merit, then that fact may be used to discredit future complaints by the disgruntled employee.

Following Through on Complaints

Barbara, an employee at one company, complained of sexual harassment by another employee, Kevin, who was of a different race. The workforce was organized and there was a grievance and arbitration procedure in place so that no action could be taken against Kevin without evidence. Barbara claimed that her distress was so great that she needed time off from work to recover psychologically, and this request was granted up to the point where she failed to satisfy management that more time was needed (after the lawsuit was filed Barbara claimed that she had been physically threatened by Kevin). While Barbara was on leave, a supervisor was dispatched to investigate the claim within the plant.

The supervisor found nothing that was definitive enough to resolve the issue because Kevin also accused Barbara of sexual banter and of bragging about her recent performance at a strip club during an "amateur night," which could have been construed as an invitation to engage in talk about sexual matters. In fact, the investigation indicated, the problem was simply that both employees had become antagonistic toward each other. If they had been of the same sex, they might well have fought it out off-premises.

Barbara had given a written statement early on, but it was composed off-premises and was not reviewed with her personally to resolve ambiguities or to resolve the issues raised by the in-house investigation—the question of whether or not she had some degree of culpability in provoking any untoward remarks. There was a need for Barbara to return to the premises for further questioning or for management to meet with her off-site. The employer tried to schedule an appointment at the plant, but Barbara never came back to meet. No follow-up action was taken such as setting up an off-site meeting or even writing her to explain the need for further investigation.

Later, Barbara was discharged after she failed to return to work or provide acceptable medical justification for her prolonged absence. Discharge was premature because the investigation had not been finished, it had come to a halt awaiting Barbara's return to work. There was every reason to complete the investigation to determine if Kevin deserved discipline for harassment, sexual or otherwise. Imagine how cavalier the employer would look at trial if it did not put the issue to rest, it would be as if they did not know or care that a harassment problem might exist. This is especially true because at that time, there was no compelling need to fire Barbara.

Barbara sued, claiming "pretextual discharge" asserting that she could not return to work because the sexual, and possible physical, harassment issues remained unresolved. She asserted that she was physically afraid to return to the workplace for fear of the other employee, all of which contributed to her sensitive psychological condition. The case was ultimately settled.

What more could have been done? The company should not have permitted a loose end, in the form of the unresolved complaint, to dangle. The complaint should have been resolved before the complaining employee was fired or had an excuse to quit and claim constructive discharge. A manager could have offered to visit Barbara to finalize the investigation; if she refused that request, it would have become another factor the company could have relied upon in its defense. Alternatively, the uncertain results of the fact-finding investigation might have been spelled out in a letter to Barbara, in which she could have been told that the company needed her response on certain specific points so that it could make an appropriate decision and take any necessary action. The company could have also made self-serving remarks in correspondence with Barbara about the need for evidence from her stating that because this was a union plant and any discipline administered to Kevin would be subject to the grievance and arbitration process and the discipline could not be sustained without proof. Had this been a non-union facility the employer could have explained that because of potential discrimination issues further investigation was required. At the very least, before the employee was fired for failing to return to work, the employer should have demonstrated—by written communication—its attempt to investigate the charge. If that had been done, then Barbara would have been given clear notice that the problem was being examined and that her cooperation was essential to the ultimate resolution of the issue. This would have also precluded Barbara's claim that she was in "limbo" because she had not been told of any corrective action taken by the company to ensure her of a proper workplace. It would also have underscored her unwillingness both to cooperate and to return to work.

While it is not a legal requirement for the company to engage in greater follow-through the failure to tie up "loose ends" would have been a factual burden at trial. Had there been follow-through, the burden would have been greater on the employee to justify her failure to cooperate rather than the employer. My firm never tried this case (since it was settled), but we believed that we had a successful defense. Nevertheless, nothing in litigation is guaranteed, and we would have been much more comfortable if we could have shown that the company had gone the extra mile to get Barbara's responses to the accusation that she was as much to blame as Kevin. Barbara's response would have helped determine the extent of her responsibility in the matter.

It's Not Only What You Say But How You Say It

What you say to an employee in your writings is important. Sometimes it pays to state the facts in a cold but objective manner. This is usually true in cases of active misconduct. But what about situations involving layoff, demotion, or other circumstances where the employee cannot perform the job up to expectations? When the employee is not guilty of bad conduct but merely inept your writing should take a softer tone, while not omitting the facts favoring the company's decision. This is especially true when the employee may be the object of sympathy because of race, sex, disability, or some other protected status.

Suppose you have an employee in a protected category who has amply demonstrated his inability to perform his job correctly, so that your need to remove him from that job is manifest and immediate. The employee has successfully performed at less-demanding jobs and is not a disciplinary problem. He might thus perform other, lower-skilled jobs in your organization, but giving him such a job would require you to terminate another employee holding that job. You have no desire to do this simply to accommodate the worker who is not performing. Assume further that there is no union contract impeding your freedom to act. Do you summarily fire this guy? No! Instead, you should discharge him with a letter that reflects favorably upon your decision. For example, you could write:

> In the last twenty-four months, you have been responsible for production errors that have cost this company thousands of dollars and at least once created a substantial safety hazard that might have injured many employees. We know that you have tried to perform the job at an acceptable level, and we have tried to work with you so that you could successfully fulfill your job responsibilities, but we have reluctantly concluded that this is not the job for you. It may be that you can perform a less-demanding job, but because we have no open jobs in less-demanding positions at this time, we must terminate your employment. In the event a position opens up in the next [x] months that we believe you are qualified to fill, you will be offered that employment opportunity.

The final sentence in the letter is an example of your showing your good faith.

This letter shows a number of things:

- The employee cost the company thousands of dollars in work errors.

- The employee was a safety risk to other employees.

- Management had worked with him to try to help him succeed.

- There are no other jobs available that he might be able to perform, but if one opened up in the near future, he would be recalled to work.

Such a letter serves the purpose of stating unequivocally why the employee has been terminated as well as the fact that the company has attempted to locate less-demanding employment for him within the organization. People now may see that the employee was a problem and that you have not been totally cold-hearted and dismissive of him as a human being; indeed, he may yet regain status as an employee. If you later offer the employee a position when one opens up and he refuses it, that act undermines any sympathy he may attempt to garner by reason of his unemployment. If he ultimately accepts a lesser position in your company, fails to perform, and is discharged again, that failure reinforces the appropriateness of both the original and subsequent discharge decisions.

Employer's Legal Pad—Chapter Three Checklist

Prompt corrective action is a key to avoiding legal disputes down the road. The longer you allow inappropriate behavior to exist, the greater your chance of facing a lawsuit.

- Require employees to write and sign a "State of Employment" form so they can review the company. Such an employee review may help you identify potential problems.

- Reference any problems or complaints in employee reviews, and hold on to those reviews as you may need them years later.

Be aware of the tone of your communications, especially when dealing with employees who have done no wrong but may face a lay-off, demotion, loss of overtime, or other cutbacks.

CHAPTER FOUR

Communications Strategies to Help You Avoid Legal Woes

Back in the days when union organizing drives were far more frequent than they are now, the employers who proved to be the most vulnerable were those that were caught by surprise when a representation petition was filed with the National Labor Relations Board seeking certification of the union as the exclusive bargaining representative of the employees. On the other hand, managers (or their subordinates) who frequently went out into their businesses and mingled with the employees knew most of what was going on and were seldom surprised. This underscores the importance of maintaining good communications with your employees.

This chapter covers critical internal communications that help identify potential problems, help avoid lawsuits in the first place, and—if a case must go to court—provide you with a solid defense.

Maintaining a Presence with Your Employees

You cannot afford to stay in your office concerned only with the core business. Instead, you must have a "presence" among the workforce.

If you can't be out there listening to workers for yourself, then you must condition your managers and supervisors to relay unusual and suspicious activities to you. It may even be worthwhile to meet regularly with your employees to review nonbusiness-related events, such as rumors and gossip, that are happening in the workplace. In these litigious times, employers should pay close attention to the grapevine.

Conditioning first-line supervisors to be alert to potential problems, not to mention communicating their concerns to their supervisors, is no easy task. After all, most supervisors know that they might be criticized because the events happened in the first place. More significantly, they know that reporting an event may require them to take disciplinary action or otherwise deal with a subject that makes them personally uncomfortable. Almost no one likes to confront others or take corrective action. It is the most reasonable thing in the world for supervisors and managers to want to put off distasteful tasks, especially talking about things that make them uncomfortable, or avoid them entirely. Dealing with sexual issues and interactions between employees may be particularly distasteful to frontline supervisors. These are the very things, however, that often lead to litigation; putting one's head in the sand only makes it worse.

Putting off what needs to be done in a timely manner creates unnecessary problems in the future. For these reasons, first-line supervisors must be aware of the need to be alert and to report what they see or hear about, all in an atmosphere that rewards them for their vigilance.

One case my firm dealt with involved Ruth, a production worker who was having problems with her second marriage. Jake, a coworker, often talked to Ruth and other workers about sex-related matters. Ruth later claimed his sexual innuendos and outright salacious comments were offensive, but she admitted she never reported these comments to management.

Jake's actions were definitely dubious. On one occasion, he carved a replica of male genitalia out of a soft material used in production and showed it to everyone who would look, male and female alike, an act that offended several employees, a fact that the company discovered to its discomfort during depositions. On another occasion, he carved an anatomically correct male and female torso and pelvis, which he and Ruth strapped on. They made a spectacle of themselves by displaying the handiwork to everyone—including Carl, the area foreman, who did nothing. Finally, Jake allegedly exposed himself to Ruth. Ruth went to the union and reported Jake's action, the union did nothing, and certainly did not tell management, because Jake was also a member. Ruth quit the company and sued, claiming constructive discharge by reason of sexual harassment.

Keep in mind that it is the employer's responsibility in harassment cases to take appropriate action designed to put an end to the harassment. The key words of the applicable case law are "action reasonably designed to stop the harassment." The law does not require 100 percent effective action. It does require reasonable steps in the right direction, along with appropriate follow-up. Further, if the company did not know of Jake's actions, the law would not impose liability because an employer is not responsible for the acts of a rank-and-file employee unless it is shown that the company knew or should have known of the misconduct or had failed to publish a policy outlawing harassment and providing a reporting procedure.

In the case of Ruth and Jake, the only thing that held the company liable was the fact that Carl, the foreman, had seen Jake's carvings and was aware of some of his sexual banter but had done nothing to put a stop to the flagrantly offensive conduct. Carl hadn't even reported Jake's actions to his superiors.

Was Ruth truly offended by Jake or was this somehow related to the separation from her husband? She claimed that her failure to report the matter was prompted by her fear of Jake and the union. That failure would have been a valid defense for the company in the absence of Carl's knowledge that Jake had engaged in gross and patently unacceptable conduct. But Carl's knowledge was sufficient to pose a factual issue that had to be decided by a jury. Even though the plaintiff's case was weak, Jake's conduct was so outrageous that no one could predict what a judge or jury might do upon trial. As a result, the case was settled. Jake, by the way, was discharged as soon as the facts came out in litigation and, of course, the client followed all the right steps before the discharge took place.

What was the company's responsibility in the circumstance? It had to take reasonable action designed to stop any sexual harassment. Had the foreman put a stop to Jake's actions or reported him so that more responsive managers could deal with the problem, Ruth would have had no claim against the company that would withstand a defense motion for what is called "summary judgment." Summary judgment is one measure a defense attorney can take to seek dismissal of a case before trial. The attorney shows, by affidavit and documents, a deposition, or other sworn proof that there is no material dispute of facts and that under the undisputed factual circumstance, the defendant is entitled to a favorable judgment as a matter of law.

In a harassment case, summary judgment could be available where the employer has taken reasonable action in a timely manner. In fact, had prompt and appropriate action been taken in the case of Ruth and Jake, it might not have been necessary to fire the offending employee. However, matters had gotten completely out of hand by the time responsible officials in the company became aware of the problems, and the company had no other choice than to discharge.

Remember, however, that even if there is no knowledge of particular circumstances on the part of management, the employer may still be liable if it "should have known" about what was taking place on its premises between employees. Does this mean that managers must go among their employees to observe what is going on? In all likelihood, the answer a court would impose would be "Yes." Therefore, supervisors and managers gain nothing by avoiding knowledge about what is happening in the workplace. That's why all supervisors and managers must understand that good communication involves listening, speaking (or writing), and *not* turning their head away.

Further, employers are automatically held liable for actions constituting harassment of their subordinates by persons in authority, such as supervisors and managers. This is known as "vicarious liability." Because the law imposes strict liability for the acts of supervisors and managers, their superiors should make an effort to be aware of offending interactions within their subordinate departments. Technically, employers are held liable for the acts of persons in a direct line of authority over the employee as opposed to managers in a different department or line of authority. However, do not become obsessed with this distinction because it is always difficult when in litigation to distance the supervisor or manager from the employee. A far better practice is to ensure that all persons in authority behave in an appropriate manner. In short, the "not in the line of authority" defense is a last-ditch defense you should not have to rely upon to avoid liability.

Publishing a Sexual Harassment Policy

Even if you maintain a presence among your employees and know what is going on with them, problems involving harassment issues may arise. Most managers are aware of a need to publish a policy against sexual harassment. (A sample of such a policy appears in Appendix F.) Because harassment may be unlawful for other reasons such as race, ethnicity, and disability, I usually advise clients not to limit the title of the policy to sexual matters because that seems to exclude other forms of unlawful harassment. It is better to make the harassment policy all-inclusive, naming all forms of unlawful discrimination and even conduct that may not be unlawful but may be interpreted as "harassment." This way, employees are on notice that any form of harassment—even if it is not unlawful—can be reported, either to their supervisor or another person within the company, and will result in discipline. The people to whom reports can be made should include someone out of the employee's line of supervision in case one or more of those supervisors is the problem.

Interpreting Employee Behavior

Alert supervisors and managers can be a blessing. In one of my cases, a dismissed employee named Don filed a claim that he had been dis-criminatorily fired because he was disabled. That claim was without legal merit and we were in the process of proving it when Don filed a new, second charge claiming that he had been unable to secure other employment because his former supervisor, Earl, had given him a "negative reference." The problem presented here is the fact that even if the original charge is without legal merit and is dismissed by the court or agency, the very fact that a charge was made in the first place is a legally protected activity and enables the charging employee to claim that he was retaliated against merely because he filed the charge. (In short, the law encourages the employee to file a charge even in questionable circumstances by granting him legal protection.)

Don's second charge alleged that the so-called negative reference was an unlawful act of retaliation because he had filed the previous

charge of disability discrimination. To prove that he had been victimized by reason of a negative reference, Don secured a written statement from a sympathetic business owner, John. In a written
statement, John declared that he had refused to hire Don because Earl
had given him a bad recommendation in a telephone conversation. A
telephone conversation between John and Earl had taken place, although the content of the conversation was disputed. Earl vigorously
denied having given Don a negative reference.

Before the trial took place, Earl kept his eyes open and spotted
Don's car parked at John's place of business for weeks on end. When
John was deposed, it was discovered that he had been on friendly
terms with Don for several years and had actually hired Don for several
weeks despite the alleged negative reference and his written statement
that he had refused to hire Don. This admission contradicted John's
statement and discredited both him and Don, who—it turned out—
had also failed to report his earnings at John's business. Needless to
say, this also severely impacted the credibility of Don's claim that he
had received a negative reference. It also affected the Don's claim for
lost wages from his original job. Upon trial John did receive a small
verdict in his favor but not nearly so large as what might have been
rendered. We believed the jury was split on the issue so that the small
verdict was a compromise that allowed the jury members to agree and
dispose of the case with finality.

Here's another case that shows the importance of interpreting employee behavior. Some years ago, before sexual harassment became a
recognized cause of action, I defended a discharge case for a defense
contractor where the manager, Bill, had become fed up with the she-
nanigans of an employee named Ernie. Bill effectively used progressive
discipline with Ernie, eventually made a case, and recommended discharge. The company fired Ernie following Bill's recommendation,
and Ernie promptly sued the company.

Ernie and Bill were both African American but that did not resolve the claim of racial discrimination. The case was tried before a jury based on a claim that the discharge violated the Civil Rights Act of 1866. (This law was used instead of the EEOC and Title VII of the Civil Rights Act because those laws did not provide for a jury trial and the 1866 law did. The Supreme Court eventually found that the 1866 law did not apply to discharge cases, but Congress has since amended the law so that jury trials pursuant to that statute are once again available.) From the outset of the trial, Ernie's attorney had his wife and children enter the courtroom and stay for the proceedings. Ernie's attorney made a point of claiming that the discharge had resulted in emotional distress to the plaintiff because he was a "family man" and was no longer able to support his family through his earnings.

The company's human resources director, who assisted me during the trial, told me that Ernie made a point of pestering a female co-worker, Ellen, telling her that he would take her out and show her a good time and that if she "went black she would never go back." (This was well before the concept of sexual harassment developed.) After the second day of the trial, I interviewed Ellen and she confirmed what I had been told and then some. A married woman, Ellen was incensed at Ernie's gall and willingly testified to all that had happened when they worked together. As Ellen told of her experiences with Ernie, his wife looked on in amazement, and before Ellen was through with her testimony, the wife left the courtroom. Ernie's attorney stomped the floor and tried to demean Ellen, implying that she was promiscuous, but this was to no avail. The jury returned a finding for the employer on the first ballot.

It is not mere idle curiosity to seek out the interactions between employees (and between employees and supervisors). Men and women seldom coexist in the same work area without friction or relationships developing that sometimes generate even more friction. Employees may pull inappropriate pranks. Offensive nicknames may crop up. When company rules are enforced only sporadically, a supervisor who wants to discipline a worker in a protected category may find that the company is vulnerable to a charge of discriminatory rule enforcement. Things happen, and you may not be able to stop all of them. But if you communicate effectively with your employees and become aware of potential issues, you have a chance to stop problems before they get out of hand by taking appropriate remedial action in a timely fashion.

Employer's Legal Pad—Chapter Four Checklist

Internal communications, including listening, can make a dramatic difference in resolving conflicts before they boil over into the legal realm.

- Get out there in your workplace (or assign someone to get out there for you) and understand the conditions and the context in which litigation might happen.

- Listen to employees, and act on complaints in a timely manner.

- Train managers and supervisors to speak up about problem employees and potential legal problems sooner rather than later, and reward them for their vigilance.

- Don't put off a difficult conversation because the subject matter makes you uncomfortable. You are only delaying the inevitable and potentially making matters worse.

CHAPTER FIVE

Investigating Problems and Preserving Evidence

Employment law cases are usually far more factually intensive than law intensive. This means that if you garner all of the facts concerning the issue, you increase your chances of either avoiding a lawsuit altogether or, if there is a lawsuit, of prevailing. Furthermore, when an employee, supervisor, or manager comes to you with a concern, it is usually far less expensive for you to gather and organize all of the facts yourself than to hire an attorney to do the job. Many times, I, a partner, or an associate have been called upon to investigate and document the defense of a charge or lawsuit, a service for which we must charge. This cost often exceeds the charge for the actual trial because by the time of trial, many of the facts have been winnowed out as irrelevant or dismissed in the summary judgment stage.

This chapter will step you through the process of gathering and preserving evidence. Remember, your goal here is to avoid getting sued and having to go to court. When good internal communications lead to a thorough and timely investigation, the evidence itself often convinces a plaintiff to drop her claim.

Investigations

Even if you have employment liability insurance, the attorneys hired by the insurance carrier will rely on you to present the facts. That's because insurers don't like to pay their attorneys to investigate, only to present a defense. In addition, insurance companies do not insure you against punitive damages, and punitive damages are the iceberg beneath the surface in a discrimination case. Virtually every court pleading filed by an employee-plaintiff seeks punitive damages. Insurance also does not protect you from orders of reinstatement or promotion, which you may face if you lose a case. The usual way out of such an order is to reach a monetary settlement out of court, a burden that an insurer may not be obliged to assume.

There are a number of parts to a proper investigation. A proper investigation means that you talk to witnesses, interview the offending employee (protecting that person's privacy to the best of your ability), obtain statements (even if you have to write them yourself, as discussed later in this chapter), preserve samples of bad work, review personnel files, take photos or videotape, and do everything else you can think of in order to satisfy yourself that you are the master of the facts.

During your investigation, save all the relevant evidence you find. For example, if time cards are part of the evidence, make certain they are not destroyed (for instance, as part of an internal company document destruction policy). If poor work is at issue, try to preserve examples of the subquality work. I have preserved examples of such things as bad printing, bad proofing of printed material, poorly machined products, and the laboratory analysis of a chemical product that showed problems due to improper mixing during production and poorly manufactured end products.

Do not discard prior disciplinary reports. Just because reports are old doesn't mean they're irrelevant. These documents may show prior knowledge of forbidden acts by the employee or a history of poor performance. Plaintiff-employees want to create the impression that they have given the employer years of good service and are deserving of some latitude, even when they have erred. To counter this, you may need to show that they have given years of marginal service and have never been truly good employees. Employees claiming discrimination may not be aware that you have evidence showing that they, or others, have been similarly disciplined in the past. If you have records to show that employees in a nonprotected class have been similarly treated before, you have gone far in negating a claim of disparate treatment.

You should also preserve the job applications of employees you hire, which inquire into an applicant's previous employment history. If this inquiry is not being made, it should be. These records are important because they may assist in limiting damages. This is accomplished by showing that the employee has drifted from job to job and never worked in one place for more than a few years. For example, a forty-year-old dismissed employee may claim that he intended to work for the company until age 70 and thus seek thirty years of front pay. In reality, he never worked any one job for more than two years. Hopefully, your records show the employee to be a "drifter" from job to job, thus enabling you to counter his claim successfully or at least limit it to a shorter term of years.

Preserving the Facts

Well-preserved facts are a blessing to all people who must defend their companies. The first step in defending your company is to be well informed. Journalism students are taught that there are 5 Ws that must be known before writing a news story: *who, what, when, where,* and *why.* Here, we focus on the *who, what, when,* and *where* (*why* is discussed in Chapter Six).

You must know the *who, what, when,* and *where* of every case. There are times when you have to rely on your attorneys for help with this. Often, on the eve of a trial, they know the facts better than the witnesses because the attorneys have poured over written statements and other evidence to the point of memorization, whereas the witnesses may have forgotten things that happened months or years before. The preserved evidence makes it possible to refresh witnesses' memories so that they can credibly and honestly testify.

Remember, the plaintiff is seeking as much money as possible, and every real or imagined act of discrimination will be burned into his memory, sometimes to the point of distortion. He'll never forget what he thinks he remembers, even if the facts are more imagined than real. However, you and your people may easily forget or confuse the facts because you moved on after the event to other more important things, and your memory has grown dim. Without the means to refresh your memory, you are in trouble because you are facing a person who will remember every detail—real or perceived.

Putting Everything in Writing

The most obvious way to preserve evidence is to put everything in writing. A manager who worked for one of my clients once complained of the burden of doing so. I replied that this burden was nothing compared to the work he would have to do if an employee who was causing him problems sued the company. Supervisors and managers should be the first to give written statements. These statements should be reviewed, not for spelling and grammar, but for clarity and comprehensibility. In fact, spelling and grammatical mistakes may even lend credibility to the statement.

If the person is writing the document by hand (rather than using a keyboard), she should use ink, not pencil, so that clear copies can be made. Often these documents must be sent by fax, and documents that are not clear do not transmit well. The writer should date the statement and sign her name at the end. All statements should be written as near in time to the events as possible.

Make sure the statements include the facts as to *who, what, when,* and *where* are involved:

1. *Who.* Names should be explicit so there is no dispute about the identity of the person involved as well as the names of all witnesses.

2. *What.* What happened should be clear to a stranger to your company reading the statement on a completely cold basis.

3. *When.* The statement should be dated so that it is clear when the event happened.

4. *Where.* The statement should specify the place or places where events occurred.

Witnesses, including both employees and managers, should be asked to sit down and write up what they heard, saw, or may have said, following the principles just outlined. (Remind witnesses, not the offender, that they will not face any retribution for making their statement.) This should be done even if you must pay overtime to keep an employee on site to make a statement. If that is not possible, have the employee bring the written statement to you the next day. If you cannot conduct the investigation yourself and you have doubts about the ability or experience of the person who is doing it, it may be a good idea to write out a script of questions for her to ask the witnesses and parties involved.

Review what has been written. All too often, management puts its faith in the writings of uneducated workers after giving their statements only a cursory review, if any. Ask yourself, "If an outsider who knows nothing of our operation were to read this statement, would he understand exactly what happened?" The statement should be clear enough for the answer to be "yes."

Are the facts clearly set forth, especially concerning the operative event? Are names named? Are dates and times correct? What about the location of events and other witnesses? What was done to offend the employee or supervisor, or what other transgression occurred? What reaction did the offended employee or supervisor have? If one person made a statement, did the other person reply, and if so, what was said? The more you do to preserve evidence that is contemporaneous with the event, the greater the accuracy of your investigation. The more you do, the less you must pay a lawyer to do for you.

Remember that you can write the statements out for witnesses and have them sign off, but this is not preferred. If the statement is in their own hand (grammatical warts and all), they will have trouble later denying the fact that they authored the statement. Subsequent claims on their part that you "made" them write it are hard to sell to a fact finder.

Getting It in Their Own Words

Witness statements do not have to harmonize exactly, but if there are discrepancies in the main points, sit down with each witness to find out why that difference exists. There are various reasons why there may be discrepancies:

- Someone may not have been present at all times.

- The witness may have been present only at the start or the finish of the event.

- The witness may not have been able to hear all that transpired over surrounding noise.

The statements should be amended, if necessary, by the witnesses themselves to account for these differences. This can be done in a separate document or by an attachment to the original statement. If any differences cannot be reconciled, then those differences demand investigation that enables you to make a reasonable conclusion about what really occurred.

In one of my cases, there were four witnesses to an employee's misconduct. The supervisor wrote up a disciplinary report and had each witness sign off on his written statement to show agreement. This was a good move, but at the deposition, none of the four remembered events in exactly the way the supervisor had written them in the disciplinary report. None of the differences were fatal, but the witnesses had an awkward time when the plaintiff's attorney questioned them about the differences between their personal recollections and the account that they had signed. All of this made the witnesses uncomfortable and susceptible to suggestion from the plaintiff's attorney, which detracted from their credibility. As in most cases, all that was necessary was that the witnesses recall the essential facts in much the same manner. Had each witness written his own statement and management had reviewed those statements for basic consistency, the witnesses would have been more comfortable and positive in their responses.

Recollection of the exact words spoken during an incident need not be the same as long as they are similar in tone and content. In addition, times of occurrence may vary slightly. One witness may recall something that another does not remember. Bear in mind that credibility is everything in an employment law case. Remember also that witnesses are uncomfortable enough simply testifying in a case, and every bump in the road tends to upset them even more. However, if they are confident in the facts, as preserved by their own writing, they can be prepared to deal with any minor discrepancies between their recollection and that of others. They simply have to show that they did not hear all that was said or see all that was done or give whatever explanation might account for the difference between statements.

Another reason for having witnesses draft their individual observations is the fact that a witness can turn against you at some later time. In one situation, Ed, the supervisor on the night shift, brought a rank-and-file employee, Dean, in to be a witness to a disciplinary layoff of another employee, Frank, because there were no other supervisors present. Having a witness was a great idea; however, problems occurred. During the administration of the layoff, Frank became angry and vented his displeasure in an unacceptable manner by throwing things around the office. When this latest misconduct was reported to the site manager, it led to Frank's dismissal. Here, like the previous example, Ed did all of the writing describing the acts of misconduct, and Dean, the employee-witness, merely signed off on the document, apparently in agreement with Ed's written statement.

Later, Dean became a problem employee himself and was fired. Dean's sympathies then flowed to Frank. In fact, it occurred to the client that Dean wanted to sue the company over his discharge. In any event, Dean did his best to undermine the statement he had signed. Instead of confirming Ed's version of events, Dean sought to minimize what had occurred by saying that nothing was thrown; instead, he now said, Frank had only dropped something on the desk that subsequently fell on the floor by accident. Dean then claimed that the report was "incorrect" and grossly overstated the misconduct that had occurred. When asked to explain just why he had signed the report if it was inaccurate, Dean stated that he signed off only because Ed told him that the differences between what had happened and what was in the written report were insignificant. Once again, a trial problem was created that could have been avoided.

If Dean had put his account in his own hand, in his own words, it is very unlikely that his statement would have differed in any significant way from Ed's. Indeed, how credible would Dean (or any witness) have been if he testified that he only wrote what he was told to write? If Dean had the temerity to testify that he wrote a false statement because he was ordered to by Ed he would impair his credibility before both a court and jury because he would then be implicating himself as a co-conspirator in the discipline, so to speak. Further, he would have a lot of explaining to do if he did not retract his statement as soon as he was free from Ed's influence. Of course, Dean could have made such a claim, but it takes a hardened perjurer to tell a bald-faced lie, contradicting his own written statement, when he is in a court of law and under oath. Few witnesses are bold or stupid enough to try! Furthermore, only the most credulous of jurors would believe such a tale.

What do you do if the witness cannot or will not write out a statement? In such a case, you must interview the witness and take down her statement as she relates events or answers your questions. Remember, this is not a paper you are writing for freshman English class in hopes of getting a good grade. Take the statement down in the person's own words, using colloquialisms, spoonerisms, bad syntax, and all. If the witness agrees to sign the statement you have drafted, have her sign the bottom of each page and initial each correction. If she will not sign the statement, you can attest to what you were told, and the recitation will sound enough like the witness that she will likely not deny having made the statements contained therein. If she does, she will probably not be believed.

Confronting the Employee with the Facts

Now that you have the supervisor's statement and the witnesses' statements, what do you do? The next step is to confront the offending employee with the offense and the facts against him. At this point, you must exercise judgment whether or not to confront the employee with all facts or just the ultimate facts. Then the employee should be given an opportunity to state his defense or excuse. In labor arbitration, this is called "due process," and some arbitrators require that it be done or they will overturn an employer's discharge decision on the grounds that it was not for "just cause" under the terms of the union contract. This concept has crept into the psyche of U.S. workers and juries alike, so it cannot be dismissed lightly.

As difficult or unnecessary as this step may seem, it is truly a good idea to confront the offending employee. This is a valuable step in the disciplinary process in employment law cases, as well as in labor cases where the discipline is contested pursuant to a grievance and arbitration procedure. It is a demonstration that you were not arbitrary in your treatment of the employee and that you made an effort to be fair and gave her a chance to be heard. Judge Roy Bean, the nineteenth-century judge known as "the law west of the Pecos," always proclaimed that he gave defendants a "fair trial before they were hung." You should do no less, even if you are reasonably certain of the ultimate decision at the time you confront the employee.

There are times when an employer may not want to disclose the names of witnesses. The giving of names is often unnecessary because it is the facts that the employee should be confronted with and given the opportunity to contest. It may also be unnecessary to disclose each and every fact to the employee. What must be done is to confront the employee with the "ultimate" facts that constitute the charge against him.*

I can recall one instance in which an egregious lawsuit might have been avoided had there been discussion with the employee before adverse action was taken. While the case did not involve a discharge, it did involve a change in a salesperson's commission rate. The salesperson, Tony, was growing older and more ineffectual by the day, and the owner of the company decided to change the commission rate and did so in a manner that diminished Tony's earnings considerably. Tony found out about the change and promptly sued for breach of contract.

During the case Tony produced a handwritten promise of a commission rate signed some forty years before by the previous president and owner of the company. That document had never been revoked or formally amended in writing; indeed, there was no copy of the document in the company's records. The company had every right to change the commission rate without the employee's consent as long as the employee was notified first. State law provided that with notice,

---

*Some states require employers to give employees access to their personnel files under certain circumstances. This may give the employee a chance to learn the full scope of your investigation, depending upon the statute and the timing of the request to inspect the file.

if the employee continued working under the new commission rate, he would be deemed to have accepted the reduction. The problem that arose was the fact there had been changes in the commissions paid over the forty-year period, and there was no proof that Tony had ever been notified in advance of the change. Further complicating the case was the fact that Tony had no particular means of verifying the results of his sales efforts that the company could use to show that Tony must have known of the change. Tony claimed he was unaware of all of these changes because his commission rate was always calculated by the employer, he had never questioned that calculation. This left Tony able to claim, which he did, that he was not aware of the fact that commissions had been underpaid from the original rate he was promised for many years. The failure of the company to keep adequate records and to justify the basis for commissions paid over the years prevented the company from proving that Tony knew or should have known that his commission rate had changed and that he legally accepted the change by continuing to work. The failure to sit down and discuss the matter with Tony in advance of the actual reduction in commission rate resulted in an abrupt change that Tony resented, for obvious reasons. A detailed meeting would have at least given the company advance notice of the issues raised by Tony's civil action and an opportunity to try to mollify Tony before he got mad and quit. That resentment led to a breach of contract civil action that disclosed past commission payments that allegedly conflicted with the written promise of commissions. The consequent bad feelings produced litigation, a jury trial that resulted in a hung jury, and ultimately a settlement to compromise the claim before a second trial took place. Had there been a conciliatory meeting with Tony, all of the information unknown to present management might have been discovered as well as the apparent unilateral change in the commission rate.

Dealing with Difficult Witnesses

Another possible problem that might occur during your investigation is posed by the employee who wants his lawyer present during an investigatory interview. Employees have no right to have an attorney present if the employer is a private company. (State and federal employers may have some obligation to permit legal representation depending upon the circumstances.)

What about the employee who wants another employee present for the interview? If the employee is protected by a union contract, he has every right to have his union steward present, or a fellow employee in the absence of a steward. A nonunion employer does not need to permit another employee to be present. However, if the accompanying employee is competent and has no ax to grind, it may not do any harm to allow her to be present. You may also turn the witnessing employee's presence to your advantage by having her write a simultaneous report on the facts disclosed at the meeting and the comments of the participants. The witness's statement should be reviewed with the witness to ensure accuracy. Whenever possible, you should also have a management-side witness present so that you are not the victim of the two-witnesses-against-one-witness scenario.

There can be exceptions to every rule. When the employee's actions have been so outrageous and notorious that there is no room for doubt, you may not need to confront the employee with the accusations against him. However, in most instances, the employer has much to gain and nothing to lose by giving the employee a chance to explain himself. From time to time, you will find an excuse or explanation in justification of the offense that alters the decision you might have made. You may also find that employees of different races or sexes have, in fact, received different treatment. You might even find that the employee is not the guilty party. It is therefore recommended that you confront the employee and if exception is to be made it is limited to the most clear-cut and outrageous circumstances.

In all events, document what the employee tells you at this time so that if he changes his story later on, you have an oral or written statement that may be used to discredit him. It is an even better idea to have the employee put his excuse or defense in writing. Belated excuses for misconduct hurt the employee's claim when you can prove the excuse is an afterthought and was never presented to the employer before discipline. The problem that may arise is proving that the excuses are belated. Nothing proves this better than having the employee's written statement that fails to mention any new excuse, giving you room to argue that his excuse or explanation is nothing more than post-discharge nonsense.

What do you do if the offending employee refuses to cooperate? Clearly, you cannot restrain an employee during the investigatory process. Instead, you must advise him that in the absence of his cooperation, you must make a decision based upon the facts known to you at that time. The fact that you gave notice to the employee of the consequences of non-cooperation and the employee's uncooperative attitude should be documented so that these things may be demonstrated in the event of future litigation.

The Case of the Jerk of a Manager

One case that I tried does not involve an employee's excuse but demonstrates the value of having the employee's relevant statements in writing. The employee, Ken, was a supervisor who had been demoted. Ken claimed that the manager, Vincent, acted out of racial animosity. As proof, Ken cited numerous complaints, but they did nothing to prove racial discrimination because Vincent was a real jerk of a manager and abused all subordinate employees and supervisors equally. (Indeed, one Caucasian supervisor even suffered a nervous breakdown at Vincent's hands.)

However, Ken had an ace in the hole: his claim that Vincent had directed a racial epithet at him on one occasion. This would have meant that there would likely have been a swearing match in court, except that the company fired Vincent long before trial. When it came time to get his deposition, his whereabouts were unknown and we could not find him to elicit a denial from him that he used the racial slur. The only thing that saved the company was that Ken had made numerous complaints in great detail in writing about Vincent's actions and never once made reference to the racial epithet being uttered. He was also interviewed by Vincent's manager who had received complaints from Ken and during the interviews he had never referenced the alleged racial slur. The court discredited Ken because if Vincent had in fact uttered such an obvious slur, there could be little doubt that Ken would have referenced it in his written communications as well as reported it in his conference with Vincent's manager.

Knowing the Employee's Excuse

Knowing the employee's excuse also plays a valuable role in determining discipline. You should ask the following questions:

1. Is the excuse worthless?

2. Is the excuse a reason for moderating what would otherwise be the penalty?

3. Is there no excuse?

4. Did the employee show or fail to show remorse?

5. Was the employee dishonest or disingenuous in his excuse?

Any number of these things can be cited when you state the reason for your ultimate decision. At the very least, this kind of investigation shows that you investigated the events and considered the employee's defense before you took adverse action.

Another reason to have the employee put in writing whatever explanation or excuse he offers is to make him commit himself to his version of events. Discharged employees often try to work around the employer's stated reasons for discipline. Once the employee has committed himself to a defense and that defense is documented, he cannot easily change it to contest a valid disciplinary decision. In other words, as my late partner Lee McMahon used to tell me, "His lips are sealed." It is amazingly easy to secure the employee's explanation in written form; usually, all you have to do is ask. If the employee refuses, make sure you document this refusal.

My son was working as a store manager in a city notorious for its litigiousness when, in his absence, an employee took several hundred dollars from the till. My son confronted the employee and asked him to explain his actions in writing. The employee complied; in writing, he admitted the theft, acknowledged that he expected to be fired, and then left without further ado. The owners of the store were surprised and grateful that the employee was dismissed so easily and without expensive repercussions.

Finally—and I cannot emphasize this too strongly—by giving the employee a chance to defend himself, you have shown that you have treated the employee with dignity, treated him like a human being of value, and not discarded him as an unworthy vassal in an imperious manner. As part of this process, there should be a gap in time between your meeting with the employee and the final disciplinary decision.

That gap can be fifteen minutes or several days. The important thing is that you be able to show that you took the time to reflect upon the facts of the matter before making the ultimate decision. Regardless of whether you are the only decision maker or a member of a committee, if you take time to reflect on the facts and the employee's excuses, you demonstrate a judicious approach to the issue.

This kind of deliberation reflects favorably upon you because juries (and judges) do not like employers who are arbitrary and capricious. If a court or jury believes the employer acted fairly in the circumstances, it may tend to find in favor of the employer even if it believes the employer's actions were harsh. If the jury believes the employer's violation of law or contract was more technical than substantive, or that the employee is not without fault, then it will tend to minimize any damage award. On the other hand, if a jury believes that an employer has acted unfairly, it will seize any rationale to rule against the employer. The more unfair the action appears in the jury's opinion, the greater the damages, punitive and actual, that will be imposed upon the losing employer.

Judges are also human and seldom act out of pure logic or legal precedent. If a judge does not like an employer's actions, there are subtle ways of undermining a defense by allowing the plaintiff-employee's lawyer to offer less than relevant evidence or even evidence the judge might otherwise determine to be inadmissible. Appellate courts will offer you no relief because they too may be influenced by an employer's negative actions. Even if they are not so influenced, they will not reverse a trial court unless its evidentiary or legal errors are so egregious that they cannot be overlooked.

Last, do not forget to document the meeting at which the disciplinary decision is discussed with the employee. Too often, I have come across manager-witnesses who failed to document their final meeting with an employee and have no real recollection of what was said at the meeting. Indeed, managers may not even recall when the meeting was held. Do not place yourself or your employer in that pathetic posture. Remember all those old saws from your youth like, "A stitch in time saves nine," and "For want of a nail, a shoe was lost." Taking the extra time to investigate, document, and preserve may well save your company time, money, and aggravation.

Employer's Legal Pad—Chapter Five Checklist

When conducting an investigation, get a statement from everyone involved. Get everyone's story, in their own handwriting, warts and all—and get it in ink!

- Keep all documents. A plaintiff will always remember everything, even though you (and your witnesses) may not.

- Don't worry about small discrepancies in people's stories. Memories may change to a degree, but when people are telling the truth, their credibility will remain intact.

- Keep in mind that spelling and grammar do not count as long as people's statements are readable. In fact, not having to worry about spelling and grammar may free people up and lend authenticity to their written statements.

- If you confront the accused, do it after you've gathered and read all the statements.

- Confront the employee with the ultimate facts, and secure his version of events, preferably in writing.

- Though prompt action is desired upon completing an investigation, take a little time to reflect before making a final decision.

Knowing Why Things Happen Strengthens Your Case

For our purposes, the *why* that the journalism student seeks to find out may not be essential (compared with the *who, what, when,* and *where*), but it should be kept in mind because it may enhance the credibility of your decision and strengthen your defense should an employee take legal action. This chapter identifies some of the common *whys* behind employee lawsuits.

Digging Deep for *Why*

Jerry, an African American lathe operator who was a union member, was on strike picketing his employer, a small Midwestern machine shop. One morning, George, the owner, stopped at the picket line on his way in and asked Jerry, "How is everything going?"

"Not so well. I'm quitting," said Jerry. "I'm only going to be picketing a few more days and then I'm going back to California." (Jerry had lived in California for many years before returning to his

65

hometown, where the company was located.) George was not un-happy with the news because Jerry was a relatively new employee and a marginal lathe operator by George's high standards.

When the strike ended, George was surprised to see Jerry return to the plant. George refused to put him back to work, telling him, "You said you quit. I took you at your word and made other arrangements for the lathe." Jerry made it clear that he considered this discrimination. He filed a grievance with the union and charges with the Equal Employment Opportunity Commission alleging race discrimination. George referred the matter to me because I was the company's labor and employment attorney. A few days later, I went to the workplace to investigate for purposes of responding to the grievance and charges.

I interviewed George and then went to speak to the people who witnessed his conversation on the picket line with Jerry. Not surprisingly, no union member would cooperate and confirm what Jerry had said about quitting. When I told George that it would be his word against Jerry's, he was adamant, saying, "I don't want him back. He said he quit and that's that." I believed George because I knew he was remarkably honest.

Fortunately, the union was content to let the grievance sit idle while the race discrimination charges were pending. After a few weeks, a right-to-sue letter was issued, Jerry found a lawyer, and the company was sued in federal court. The grievance remained unresolved.

When George was deposed, Jerry's attorney asked him, "Why would Jerry quit a perfectly good job in his hometown and move to another state?" Obviously, neither George nor I had an answer for this, but it made me think. It was clear that Jerry's attorney intended to make as much as possible out of the fact that Jerry had no reason to state that he intended to quit at a time when he was striking for a better contract. This issue would obviously be the lynchpin of Jerry's case. Jerry would no doubt be prepared to testify, as he did at deposition, "There I was on the picket line striking for a better contract. Why would I quit during a strike when it was clear that sooner or later there would be a contract and we would return to work?"

Why had Jerry wanted to quit? I thought about this and decided to see if there were any criminal or civil actions pending in which Jerry was a party. I visited the county courthouse, looked at the circuit court filings, and discovered that Jerry's wife had filed a divorce petition the day before he told George he was quitting. The divorce petition, which was served the day it was filed, accused Jerry of being a bad husband who had been mentally and physically cruel to her. This was good news for Jerry's employer, but bad news for Jerry, and it was no stretch to argue that because of the petition he might well have considered going back to California. To the extent it answered the question "why would he quit at a time when he was walking a picket line" it made George believable and put a burden upon Jerry to credibly explain why the divorce had no impact upon his future employment plans.

I tried the case before a federal court sitting without a jury (at the time, civil rights cases were tried before the court and not a jury). The judge dismissed Jerry's lawsuit because he believed George. When I met with George to go over the decision, he was happy, to say the least, but curious as well. "You thought that finding out about Jerry's wife divorcing him would be a big deal," he said. "But the judge wouldn't even let you put the divorce petition allegations in evidence. Why is that?"

I pointed out that the judge had let me establish that Jerry was sued for divorce and served the day before he said he was quitting. I explained that this was relevant to the issue presented by Jerry's attorney, which was why Jerry would quit a perfectly good job when he had no other offers of employment. The judge probably excluded the actual divorce petition, which made some ugly allegations, for fear that an appeals court might have felt he was prejudiced by the allegations. (The judge knew, like all lawyers know, that divorce petitions are often exaggerated.) "But the fact remains," I said, "that we did prove he was being sued for divorce the day before he told you he quit, and those facts destroyed the argument that Jerry had no reason to quit, leave town, and return to California. Remember, Jerry denied quitting, and your testimony that he quit voluntarily pitted your credibility against his. The judge believed you and did not believe Jerry. Because we know why Jerry said what he did, his lawyer's argument was foreclosed and your credibility enhanced because there was a reason for Jerry to say he was quitting."

The union never did take the grievance to arbitration. The moral of this story for unionized companies is try to urge the union toward inaction, or you'll have two cases to defend. The moral for all companies is to try to find out why something occurred so you'll have more information to use to defend your company.

Checking the Record

Not too many years ago, I visited a company plant to prepare for a union grievance arbitration scheduled the next day. Charley, the employee in question, had been fired for insubordination. In addition to the grievance, he had also filed a race discrimination charge over his dismissal. (More often than not, employees use every legal forum available when seeking money from their employer.)

I asked the HR manager, Bill, what happened. Bill explained that

Bob, the second-shift superintendent, was having a "toolbox" meeting at the start of his shift. Because the employees were all spread out, he asked them to move closer to him so that he could be heard over the factory noise. Charley, a one-year employee, was the only one who did not move. Bob asked Charley to move in closer so he could speak without shouting. Bob used a reasonable tone of voice, but Charley said, "No one tells me what to do. They have to ask and I will do it if I want to, otherwise I won't." Bob then asked Charley to move a second time and this time said "please." Charley then said, "I have to go pee" and left the meeting in a huff. Bob canceled the toolbox meeting and, as soon as he could, brought Charley to see Bill and the plant manager.

According to Bill, Charley began the meeting by saying, "Everything Bob says is a lie." The meeting went downhill from there, with Charley's attitude getting worse. Then, Bill said, "We fired him."

Other than absenteeism, Charley had no disciplinary record, and I could not understand why he had suddenly developed an attitude problem. I had trouble researching the case because of the usual "he said this" and "he said that" problems, which were compounded by employees who were reluctant to testify against a fellow worker. For lack of anything else to research, I looked at Charley's personnel file and was amazed by what I found. It all came out when the case went before the arbitrator.

After presenting the company's witnesses before the arbitrator, I cross-examined Charley. Here are some of the questions that were asked:

Attorney: You were being garnished $56 a week for child support for Jane Smith at the time you were fired, correct?

Employee: Yes.

Attorney: You were also being garnished by Helen Jordan for $112 a week for child support at the time you were fired?

Employee: Yes.

Attorney: You were also being garnished by Jane Gregory for $112 a week for child support at the time you were fired?

Employee: Yes.

Attorney: All three garnishments began two weeks before you were fired, correct?

Employee: Yes.

Attorney: What were your gross earnings each week before taxes?

Employee: $480 plus overtime once in a while.

Attorney: How much did you net each week after the $280 in garnishments and payroll taxes were deducted?

Employee: Not much.

Attorney: Are you now receiving unemployment compensation?

Employee: Yes.

Attorney: How much?

Employee: $240 a week.

Attorney: Is the unemployment payment being garnished?

Employee: No.

Attorney: Is it fair to say that you are financially better off not working and instead drawing unemployment?

At this point the union objected to the question. The arbitrator sustained the objection and cut me off on this point. However, the evidence of irresponsible fatherhood not only made Charley look bad as an individual but also demonstrated that he had no reason to work when he could earn more from unemployment compensation. The information was clearly relevant. The arbitrator did not want to hear any more testimony on this point because he had heard enough. The arbitrator never relied on the garnishment information to rule against Charley, but it was obviously in his mind when he began his deliberations.

The testimony of the other employees present did not help the company's case. They did not want to lie to help Charley so they equivocated. Needless to say, the arbitrator believed the testimony of Bob, the shift superintendent, and found that Charley had in fact been insubordinate and unapologetic for his conduct. The arbitrator dismissed the grievance. Once it became clear that Charley wanted to be fired so he could collect unemployment, he could not find an attorney to sue the company for race discrimination.

This case illustrates the value of checking the record and investigating every aspect of a case, including facts that management has ignored as being irrelevant in defending the claim. It shows the value of discovering the *why* of any situation.

Sometimes supervisors and managers do not consciously lie; they simply withhold facts they believe to be irrelevant or lacking a foundation for the action they want to take. Sometimes they do not know all the relevant facts. When that happens, you are not playing with a full deck of cards! This is especially true when an employee's actions do not seem to make sense or leave you wondering, "Why did she do that?" That sensation is your warning that you need to find out why the employee did what she did. You must reflect upon what you know before acting. If you have a bad feeling after acting, do not hesitate to go back and resolve any nagging questions. More often than not, you can still avoid or minimize any damage if you do not wait too long. Any time you have a troublesome, lingering doubt, take it as a signal from your subconscious that you should not take everything at face value and need to investigate further before acting.

Employer's Legal Pad—Chapter Six Checklist

Knowing what happened is essential. Knowing *why* it happened is not, but it can strengthen your defense.

- Establishing cause can be tricky. Dig down and ask probing questions to get to the heart of the matter and figure out *why* something occurred.

- Investigate every aspect of a complaint. View the alleged incident from every side.

- When you have any doubt whatsoever, do not take what you hear at face value.

CHAPTER  SEVEN

Trusting but Verifying

Sometimes an attorney learns more from cases he loses than cases he wins. This has certainly happened to me when I trusted people I should have doubted. In the course of an investigation, there may be times when a supervisor or manager lies to you or makes unwarranted assumptions. I can recall three times when I did not know the client's supervisors and/or managers were less than honest with me and I made the mistake of taking them at their word. In each case, it caused substantial harm to the defense. In each case, that harm could have been avoided had the defense been made aware of the true facts before deposition and especially before trial. This chapter looks at those three cases.

Looking for Lies

When the real facts pop up as a surprise to both the person who is lying and her attorney, the case is like a fire you are trying to put out while the plaintiff's attorney fans the flames to make the fire burn hotter. To prevent this, the decision maker should check documents, records, and the statements of all the witnesses to make certain there are no lies or unsupported assumptions. In addition, as stated in Chapter Six, if something does not seem right, you have to trust your instincts and ask questions until you are satisfied you've gotten o the bottom of things.

Take no one at his word when there are means of verifying all or part of what you have been told. In one case, we relied on the service manager of an automobile dealer to verify that a mechanic had no way to get a customer's home telephone number without the unauthorized assistance of another employee, the service writer, who was a problem employee. The mechanic had called the customer at home to solicit him for the mechanic's private repair business (to the detriment of the dealer). The mechanic was fired without legal repercussions. However, the service writer who was suspected of giving the mechanic the customer's home number was also to be the object of discipline. The service manager stated unequivocally that the write-up that was furnished to the mechanic dealt only with the items to repair and did not include the number. Moreover, the service manager indicated that only the service writer could have disclosed the number. We were suspicious of this because it did not square up with our own experience, so we questioned the service manager very carefully on this point. He maintained this position, but in the end he was flatly wrong, the telephone number was available to the mechanic and therefore we could not place exclusive blame upon the service writer. The discipline did not stand and the client lost the case.

Was the service manager wrong because he lied or because he did not know his operation very well? In either case, his accusation of a subordinate employee was worthless because it was incorrect.

The Power of the Lie

In another case, the night-shift supervisor of a manufacturing plant thought that the company wanted him to lie (which was not true) about having observed an employee engage in an act of misconduct. It would have been evident from a cursory review of the time cards that the employee was not working the same shift as the supervisor and thus could not have observed the employee. Being much younger and far more naive than I am now, I took the supervisor at his word and did not check the time cards because it never dawned on me that someone would tell such an obvious lie. Meanwhile, the opposition did subpoena the time cards, which I reviewed before production was demanded by my opponent and discovered the lie. By that time, however, it was too late: The supervisor had already perjured himself.

I confronted the supervisor after the first day of the trial. He said he thought I wanted him to lie. His lie undid the entire defense because the next day he had to be put on the stand to recant his testimony. Had the supervisor been truthful, we would have known our legal vulnerabilities and the case could have been settled with minimum expense. After the lie became evident, though, the company had no bargaining position left, could not mount a defense, and was forced to settle the case on the government's terms.

In the third case, I was prosecuting a clothing manufacturer on behalf of the National Labor Relations Board for the layoff of a number of employees who were active in organizing a union. The manufacturer's defense was that lack of business necessitated the layoff. We subpoenaed the employee time cards for the weeks after the layoff. The time cards showed that while some employees active on behalf of the union had been laid off, other employees who were not laid off were actually working overtime at time-and-a-half pay rates to make the necessary production.

We won the case handily when we proved that the overtime more than equaled the time and money saved by the layoff and that the overtime actually cost more than the cost of retaining the laid-off employees. The employer had never considered the fact that we might subpoena and review the time cards and discover the discrepancy in hours. The employer's attorneys failed to anticipate the fact that their client's was not entirely truthful with them. Because of their client's lie, or lack of candor, they had no evidence to counter the government's case. One final note: Check all company records yourself. Sometimes people will not lie but will make assumptions not warranted by the real facts and they do not bother to check the records. I once defended a company where an African-American employee claimed that he should receive a pay increase because the company had paid his predecessor, a Caucasian male, more than it was paying him. When the employee was deposed, he stated the rate of pay he thought he should receive. The employee had a contract that specified his rate of pay. I assumed the company was paying him according to the contract, and you can imagine my surprise when I reviewed the pay records that he was being paid more than the contract required. In fact, he was being paid the exact amount he claimed he should be paid! Both the employee and the company manager had no idea what the real pay rate was until the payroll records were examined. That was the end of that case.

Employer's Legal Pad—Chapter Seven Checklist

Take no one at his word when there is a way to verify what he has told you. When there is no way to verify, trust your instincts, and do so with caution and self-honesty.

- When conducting an investigation, be sure to remind witnesses to tell the truth. Make sure they know they won't get in trouble for it.

- Verify what people tell you.

- Consider time cards and electronic files as evidence of people's whereabouts.

- When checking company records, do it yourself whenever possible rather than asking someone else to do it for you.

CHAPTER EIGHT

Advantages and Pitfalls of Electronic Devices

Employers often have questions about using technology to track employees and monitor their conversations, either on a day-to-day basis or during investigations. This chapter looks at technologies that are useful for defending yourself in an employment case, especially the most valuable—a tape recorder and a videocamera.

Telephones and Tape Recorders

Federal law allows one party to a telephone conversation to record the entire conversation. It prohibits the taping of a telephone conversation by persons who are not a party to the call (see 18 United States Code §2511). State laws may prohibit the taping of a conversation without the consent of all parties. For these reasons, you must be aware of the state laws affecting your actions.

Obviously, you cannot listen in on an employee's telephone conversation when you are not a party to it unless consent or notice is given. In the latter instance, employees must be notified that their calls are being monitored. Such consent is best given in writing so that there is no doubt that consent was given.

Personally, I dislike handling employment matters by telephone if there's a chance they could become litigious. Remember the story about Earl in Chapter Four, who answered a request over the telephone from a business owner named John for an employment reference? Had that request gone unanswered or had it been answered in writing, the employee's claim that he had been harmed by Earl's negative reference would never have become a civil action.

When dealing with employees and former employees, it is far better to meet face-to-face than to have a telephone conversation. (If meeting in person is not practical, written communication is second best.) After a face-to-face meeting, it may be appropriate to confirm the details of the meeting by letter or memorandum. There are two main reasons for holding face-to-face meetings rather than telephone conversations. First, telephone conversations originated by the employer to discuss an employee's employment future may seem impersonal and cold to a jury. Second and more important, there is greater chance of miscommunication between the parties over the telephone than in a face-to-face meeting or a written communication.

Sometimes, though, there may be no good alternative to the telephone; if so, a good tape recording of the conversation may be invaluable. You should tell the other party using explicit words that the call is being recorded and ask if she has any objection. This should be done at the start of the conversation and your warning and the other party's response should be part of the recording. If she does not object, make certain that her consent is part of the recording.

If you ask for consent and it is denied, you then have several options. You may state that even without consent you are recording the conversation and the other party's option is to hang up (assuming you are not violating any state law). You may tell the other party that you will not discuss the matter over the telephone because of their objection. Finally, you may decide not to record the conversation and by that time you should have the other party on record that they do not want to be recorded. Also make certain that you have a good clean tape and that your equipment works properly because you will be discredited if there is a dispute over what was said and you have to admit in court that your tape recorder failed or the tape is inaudible. Trying to explain a tape recording gone wrong can sound like a cover-up to a judge or jury if there is any dispute about what was said.

Tapes are discoverable in litigation. By that I mean that once a civil action begins the other party may demand a copy of any recordings in your possession (this also would apply to other physical things you might possess that arguably have relevance to the case). The EEOC or any other administrative body may also make such a demand. Should you refuse to produce the recording the other party may resort to legal proceedings to compel the release of the recording. Do not record anything you are ashamed of, especially your language and tone of voice. You should have no hesitancy in giving the employee a copy of the tape, upon request, assuming you said the right things during the conversation because it shows your fairness and candid way of dealing with problems.

Be aware that you may also be recorded when conducting controversial human resources matters by telephone. In one case, a manager was recorded by her employee, and she had no written or other clear recollection of what was said during the telephone conversation. This left her at the mercy of the employee who had the tape until we got a copy of the tape during the legal proceedings.

Possibly the greatest danger of conducting human resources matters over the telephone is that if the employee places the call, he has the initiative. The employee knows the issues he wants to confront you with. You, on the other hand, may be caught unprepared and unable to give the right or best answers to questions that may be far from your mind at the time. If you are called by a disgruntled employee, do not engage in a conversation about the issues he may have. Instead, set up a time and place for meeting to discuss the issues in person. Do not hesitate to tell the employee that you want to speak to him personally and do not want to discuss matters over the telephone. At the very least, tell him that you will call him back at a later time. This delay will give you a chance to prepare yourself and possibly have someone else on the line to serve as a witness to the conversation or to make preparations to record the conversation for yourself.

Videocameras and Videotaping

Videocameras are a blessing, enabling you to demonstrate complex facts without elaborate testimony, charts, and graphs. My first experience using videotape came when a client, Juanita, was confronted by a union employee, Ralph, who wanted to return to work after settlement of a workers compensation claim. Juanita did not want Ralph back because he had suffered a ruptured vertebral disk that he chose not to have repaired. Ralph's job was physical and involved swinging a heavy sledgehammer and lifting heavy weights. Ralph would obviously reinjure himself if he returned to work.

The factual and legal problem was that Ralph had a release to return to full duty from the company doctor, Dr. Cornwall. When Juanita refused to reinstate Ralph, he filed a grievance that he had been terminated without "just cause" in violation of the union contract. The union demanded arbitration. With an arbitration hearing looming, I wrote Dr. Cornwall a detailed letter setting forth the nature of Ralph's job and asking him to reevaluate the employee's fitness. The letter did no good: Dr. Cornwall was steadfast in his opinion that Ralph could return to work, and Juanita was adamant about his not returning to the job. In desperation, I asked Juanita to videotape the job from start to finish. I then sent the videotape to the doctor, who revised his opinion and stated that the employee was unfit to return to that particular job.

When I deposed Dr. Cornwall (so that his deposition could be used in place of his actual appearance at the arbitration hearing), he testified that in his professional opinion, Ralph could not safely do the job. The doctor did not hesitate to state that his original opinion had relied on Ralph's contention during his medical exam that there were mechanical means to assist him in the performance of the heavy tasks. When Dr. Cornwall looked at the videotape, though, he realized that Ralph had not been truthful.

Juanita's judgment was vindicated when the arbitrator dismissed the grievance. Subsequently, when Ralph sued the company in state court for illegally retaliating against him because of his workers compensation claim, the trial court dismissed the claim because of the successful outcome of the arbitration. The appeals court upheld the dismissal by the trial court. Had the doctor not seen a videotape, the outcome of the case would have been very different.

More recently, an employee named Paul claimed that he had been unjustly discharged because he had sustained an on-the-job injury to his hand (which was covered by workers compensation). Paul maintained that his file had been unjustly "papered" with disciplinary reports, and part of his evidence was an allegation that he had been disciplined for not performing his job in the prescribed manner after his injury and return to work, subject to medical restrictions not relevant here. Paul claimed that the injury prevented him from doing his job properly because the work required the use of two hands; therefore, he should not have been returned to his regular job but assigned another, less demanding, job. For that reason he asserted that the discipline was unjust and could not be relied upon as a part of the employer's reason for dismissing him from employment.

During pretrial discovery, Richard—the employee who had been assigned to Paul's job after the discharge—subsequently broke his arm in an off-the-job accident but was nevertheless performing the job satisfactorily despite the cast on one arm. We videotaped Richard while he worked the job successfully, showing one of his arms clearly in a cast, and thereby belied Paul's excuse as well as proving that the employer's work expectations were not unreasonable.

E-Mail and Electronic Transmissions

Always be aware of the permanency of e-mail, instant messages, and other electronic transmissions. Do not think for one moment that your message has been wiped off the face of the earth just because you click on "delete." Many a case has hinged on a vital electronic transmission that someone thought had been permanently deleted but that was found.

Also, when e-mailing and instant messaging, people sometimes tend to be too informal and use jargon not familiar to those outside the business. You should treat e-mail with as much formality and detail as you would a letter, business report, reprimand, or any other important document. Indeed, what applies to e-mail applies to all written transmissions. Your writing should be clear and understandable to the point of simplicity. You should be businesslike when commenting on an employee's work performance, but do not let a feeling of aggravation or premature praise creep in. Write as if your message would be read by complete strangers who are sitting in judgment on your actions. If you're sued, that's what happens.

If you are dissatisfied with an employee's work, specify the problems the poor work is causing in your communication. While this is extra work for you, it may save much time in the future when you try to explain how the employee has gone wrong. For example, Ann was a plant comptroller maintaining financial records that she transmitted over the Internet. Her reports were late and sometimes in error, thereby preventing an accurate picture of the plant's performance, which in turn affected the overall company because of the need to satisfy lenders by sending them periodic reports at a specified date each month. The Vice President of Finance, Ross, sent her terse e-mails about the delays and inaccuracies using terms familiar to accountants and terms particular to certain types of intra-company documents.

Ann responded with excuses using the same type of internal jargon. Eventually Ann's failure to perform caught up with her and she was terminated. Ann sued claiming sex discrimination and sexual harassment. The company had extensive e-mail transmissions documenting the performance problems but they all required interpretation for the benefit of lay persons because they were not self-contained in the sense that the ordinary person could read them and readily discern the problems. At the trial, I had Ross explain exactly what was wrong with Ann's reports and reconcile his concerns with the messages sent her and, in turn, to translate Ann's replies. How much better it would have been had the e-mail messages been clear and self-explanatory.

In the case of Ann and Ross, we could not assume that a judge or jury would understand either the accounting involved or the effect an untimely or inaccurate report might have on the entire company. A judge or jury needs to know that financing may be jeopardized, prices may be misquoted, deliveries may be delayed, or any number of problems may be created by an underperforming and perhaps lackadaisical employee. While Ann may have understood comments Ross made to her in his e-mails, they were not obvious or clear to the rest of the world in all respects.

If you do not like what is going on with an employee, say so clearly in your written communications. State, for example, why the employee's delays or errors create a problem, even if it should seem obvious to anyone with any business knowledge. A judge and jury may not be well informed on business matters, but your well-written, clear e-mail can be used to impart that knowledge as an integral part of your defense.* In addition, the employee may get the message that you are thinking of dismissing her, and she might just improve her performance or at least get her weak excuses up front for you to negate in any follow-up e-mails.

There is another concept at work here. When you have an opportunity to put in writing criticism of an employee's performance, remember that it is an opportunity to create a document that will argue the case in your favor on countless occasions—during investigation, during discovery, during trial, and even in the jury room if the court permits exhibits to accompany jurors during their deliberations (jurors also have the right to ask to see documents should they remain in the courtroom).

In another instance, a quality manager, Fred, was critical in an e-mail of the work of a laboratory manager, Phil. Phil responded with a list of excuses. I asked Fred to investigate each excuse to determine

---

*This shows the value of creating a paper trail that may be placed in evidence in future litigation. When the paper trail contains the essence of the reason for discipline, the plaintiff-employee is placed at a great disadvantage even before his employer begins its defense.

those that could be debunked and to respond to Phil. I thought it possible that some of the excuses might be valid. Fred informed me that this was too much work for him to do. I then told him that my request was nothing compared to the work that would be generated if Phil filed a civil action. In the event of future litigation, it was necessary that Fred overcome Phil's excuses for his having failed to accomplish highly technical matters. My concern was that without detailed written communications that clearly explained the problems, a judge or jury might think that Fred's criticism was not well taken and just a pretext for discrimination.

If someone has lied to you or otherwise done something wrong, do not respond in a mean-spirited and vindictive manner in your e-mail or other writing. Simply lay out all the facts, including the harm that was done or could have been done. Write as if you are composing a letter to a layperson with no knowledge of your business. If the employee responding to your e-mail cannot produce a clear excuse for his lapses, you are getting the necessary ammunition you need to take action.

On the other side of the coin, do not be premature offering praise in an e-mail or other written communication until you are certain that it is deserved. If you must give some early expression of satisfaction, do so in conditional terms so that you do not have to reverse your decision if something goes wrong.

Handling Misuse of Company Electronics Through Monitoring

Computers and fax machines are now almost universal, and employee misuse of them is beyond dispute. It's a fact that employees use the Internet from their places of work for their own amusement and access sites that their employers do not want on the company's servers. E-mails may be sent that have nothing to do with business and may contain harassing materials or other unlawful content. Misuse of computers and company electronics may result in sabotage and actions in breach of confidentiality obligations, defamation, and copyright infringement. A clear, comprehensive, written company policy limiting the uses an employee may make of a company computer is essential. To the extent possible, employee use should be monitored and violations of policy the subject of warning or discipline.

Employers must be concerned about their employees' common law right to privacy. In addition, there are laws prohibiting the unlawful interception of electronic communications or the searching of stored electronic communications, which may affect your ability to monitor an employee free from legal repercussions. The Electronic Communications Privacy Act of 1986 (18 United States Code §2510 et seq. and 18 United States Code §2701 et seq.) regulates wiretaps and the interception of electronic communications as well as stored communications and the accessing thereof. There may well be laws in your state that also regulate these matters. There are exceptions that allow for monitoring. However, to avoid having to worry about whether or not a particular act is within some exception, it is far better to have employees consent, in writing, to the monitoring and accessing of computer information, stored or otherwise.*

A similar consent is necessary if you intend to monitor telephone and fax communications. Such individual employee consent will act as a supplement to your stated company policy (which should, of course, be communicated to all employees) and will prove that all employees

---

*Such a consent form appears in Appendix B. Note that the form has not been tested in court. You may want to review it with your attorney to be satisfied that any monitoring is protected and not in violation of either state or federal law.

are on notice of prohibited conduct and the fact that their actions may be monitored. If you intend to monitor telephone calls, your company policy should also make employees aware that they have no reasonable expectation of privacy in personal calls. If a personal call is intercepted, the employer should break his connection to the call as soon as the personal nature of the call is clear. If making personal calls is against company rules, the employer should take appropriate discipline and advise the employee that the call was not monitored once its personal nature became clear but that such calls are not allowed.

State, federal, and other government employers may have somewhat different needs in this area because of the Fourth Amendment to the U.S. Constitution, which protects the individual against unreasonable searches and seizures by government units. Government employers must therefore balance the employee's expectation of privacy against the institution's need for efficient operations. A comprehensive determination of that need must be left to the individual agency.

Monitoring the workplace with television cameras presents another issue. You should obviously not place videocameras in bathrooms, locker rooms, and other areas where the taping of employees represents an invasion of privacy not warranted by reasonable business considerations. Some states, such as Illinois, prohibit sound recordings so the monitor should capture only pictures and not sound in those states. If you have a union, you probably have to negotiate all aspects of videotaping unless the union has previously waived its right to bargain over this issue. This does not necessarily mean that agreement is required, but it does require good-faith negotiation. A good labor lawyer may be needed in the context of a union plant if agreement is not readily forthcoming.

There are other new technologies that may affect you. Global Positioning Systems are gaining wide popularity and are being used to monitor employees who must travel outside company premises. Some states, including Missouri, expressly permit or do not prohibit the tracking of cell phone signals. At this point, there is little controversy over these new technologies. However, you should check state laws and use common sense to frame a reasonable business policy so that you can prove that you are not being unnecessarily intrusive in monitoring employees.

Employer's Legal Pad—Chapter Eight Checklist

A tape recorder and a videocamera can be valuable tools in a legal defense, but they can backfire and work against an employer as well.

- You may record any telephone call to which you are a party except in some states.

- You may not record a telephone call to which you are not a party without permission.

- Avoid discussing employment decisions, especially adverse actions, over the telephone. Face-to-face is better. You should then follow up with a written memo.

- Check your state laws and/or consult your company attorney about videotaping and recording in your state.

Making Your Decision

Your investigation of an allegation by an employee, manager, or customer is complete. You've interviewed supervisors, managers, employees, and other relevant parties. Your documentation is thorough. You have accumulated relevant e-mails or legally recorded telephone calls. You have all of the facts to warrant a disciplinary action. Now it's time to deliberate. You must not only consider the facts and the statements you have gathered but you must also consider external factors.

There are certain questions you should ask and answer before taking definitive action with respect to discipline. By thinking about these questions and the answers to them, you will simplify the decision-making process:

1. What did the employee do or fail to do?

2. Why did the employee act or fail to act in the proper manner?

3. Are company rules clear? In the absence of rules, was the act clearly wrongful?

4. Does the employee have any excuse or mitigating circumstance to offer in her defense?

5. How have like or similar cases been treated in the past? If there have been such cases, what differences, if any, exist?

6. Does the employee show remorse for his actions?

7. Has the employee been honest and sincere during the investigation phase?

8. What is the likelihood that the offense will be repeated?

9. What is the employee's length of service with the company?

10. What has been the nature and character of the employee's service?

Taking the First Steps

Resolving any factual disputes and/or determining who is telling the truth is the first step. Your factual investigation should be a big help in making that determination; however, do not be deterred from making a necessary decision merely because you uncovered conflicting statements during your investigation. If you can rely on known circumstances or your own reasoned judgment to reach a decision as to what to believe, you need not be stymied in decision making.

Next, determine whether or not a rule violation was involved. Your company should have published, known rules or a published, known disciplinary procedure to help ensure consistent and fair treatment of employees. Companies that have a high level of education or achievement among employees may not have written rules but they should. Companies that have a union-organized workforce, however, need written rules so that someone cannot claim, "I didn't know *that* was against the rules." Appendix C contains a list of possible rules for you to consider, but bear in mind that it is difficult to determine every offense people are capable of committing. Any list of rules should therefore contain a catchall rule such as that shown in Appendix C, to the effect that any act considered detrimental to the company is not allowed.

What is the form of your disciplinary procedures? In all circumstances you should have a disciplinary procedure, even if it is not published. A four-step procedure is often in place for hourly workers and there is no reason that the same or a similar procedure should not be in place for the salaried or professional employee*:

1. Verbal warning

2. Written warning

3. Suspension

4. Discharge

I recommend to my clients that they do away with the verbal reprimand stage. If an act is worth criticizing, the warning ought to be put in writing at the outset; thus, you have both a first and second written warning stage. If there are matters that are too petty to justify a written warning it is a good idea for the immediate supervisor to merely speak to the employee and keep a private note of the conversation and, if minor problems continue, to then create a written warning with the aid of his notes. Any procedure you establish should reserve the right to impose discipline at any stage of the procedure, depending on the seriousness of the offense, bypassing the written stages and going to

---

*Some employers utilize a separate line of discipline for attendance policies that may have a different number of disciplinary steps.

more severe steps where warranted. Further, discipline should be cumulative so that you need not restart the disciplinary process for each separate offense. This puts the employee on notice that a subsequent offense, of any kind, may result in the imposition of the next level of discipline (or even two or three levels higher) even though that offense was different from the original offense. (Obviously, some offenses should be disciplined at the discharge or disciplinary layoff, or final warning, stage.) Supervisors should also be encouraged to keep clear notes concerning informal critiques of employee performance and actions so that they can recall these things if discipline becomes necessary.

"Stale" Offenses

Offenses that do not warrant discharge can be punished at either the first or second warning stage or by suspension, depending on the seriousness of the offense. More serious offenses can be punished by suspension or discharge. In any event, the disciplinary procedure should not require that it apply each offense independently; discipline should be cumulative with each offense proceeding to subsequent steps regardless of the violation.

At some point, lesser discipline than discharge becomes "stale" (of no value as either a legal or practical matter with the passage of time and unreliable as a credible basis for action). You may want to have a system of clearing discipline, not in the sense of removing papers from the employee's personnel file but in terms of not relying on an event that is a year or two old for the purpose of determining the appropriate level of discipline. In such circumstances, you may want to repeat the disciplinary step or start anew, depending on the time that has elapsed. By way of example, if the last disciplinary event for a minor infraction is twelve months old and the next offense is also minor, you may want to repeat the disciplinary step. If the last disciplinary event is twenty-four months old, you may want to disregard previous discipline entirely for purposes of determining the appropriate action.

Nevertheless, do not remove valid prior discipline from the personnel file. You want to prevent someone from pleading that she did not know better and be able to refute future claims of disparate treatment or show that other persons have been disciplined for the same reason in the past. You may need the evidence of prior discipline contained in personnel files.

If you are charged with or sued for employment discrimination, it is very likely that the opposing party will demand information about previous discipline. Preserving that evidence shields you from the faulty recollection of employees and supervisors alike. Moreover, if you have been consistent, this prior discipline will help you prove that your actions were not discriminatory. It is also a good idea to index disciplinary events so that you do not have to rely upon memory years after the fact or leaf through hundreds of files.

In the unlikely event you are ordered to "cleanse" an individual's file of some particular act of discipline by a court or arbitrator, you can insert the order of the court or agency insisting upon this purging into the personnel file for future reference. Then, you can transfer all removed documents to a "litigation file" maintained on a case-by-case basis. In any event, you should index and maintain a litigation file on every serious case, even if it was resolved before litigation.

Zero Tolerance

Some acts are so deplorable as to warrant discharge. There should be no hesitancy in firing someone for a legitimate reason on first offense.

However, some employers have adopted a "zero tolerance" standard for certain acts that involve something other than a willful, egregious act of misconduct. In particular, safety. As a legal counselor, I do not like zero tolerance policies except for the most serious of offenses involving deliberate acts of misconduct because such a policy removes all discretion from the manager and, invariably, some degree of judgment is required in discharge cases.

Remember that a judge or jury will not look kindly on the employer who woodenly imposes a zero tolerance policy devoid of all caring and human judgment. Zero tolerance may sound good to the boss, but it does not serve the employer well in court. This caveat about zero tolerance does not mean that some acts of misconduct should be tolerated. There is a time for discharge for the first offense, but the discharge decision should always be based upon reason and good sense as well as the rule violation.

One of my clients instituted a zero tolerance discharge rule for a failure to "lock out, tag out" electrical power before working on machinery that simply meant that when working on machinery the electric power had to be off and a lock installed to secure the switch so that power could not be inadvertently turned on while employees were engaged in maintenance work. The first person to violate the rule was a new supervisor whom the employer had gone to a great deal of time and expense to recruit. (He was a minority as well.) The supervisor was not discharged but only suspended for a few days, which made it impossible for the company to fire a rank-and-file employee committing the same offense shortly thereafter.

Recently, a New York Stock Exchange–listed company that operated a plant located in a rural area of Oklahoma had a zero tolerance policy that resulted in the discharge of a number of long-standing employees, including supervisors. The employees had firearms locked inside their vehicles, which were parked in the company lot, in violation of a no-firearms policy. Such a policy may be appropriate in a large metropolitan area, but there is an entirely different culture in the hills of southeastern Oklahoma. Of course, the company was within its rights to make such a rule, but did it have to fire several good employees with years of service? The Oklahoma legislature has since passed a law that prohibits employers from firing employees who have unloaded firearms locked in their vehicles, even on company property, and that law includes urban areas such as Tulsa and Oklahoma City. (As this is being written, other states are considering similar legislation.) The company discussed above has been the subject of legal action over the discharges.

While the previous illustrations might be a different matter if a safety rule violation resulted in injury or harm, zero tolerance policies that do not consider the willfulness of the act, its seriousness, and the harm caused can lead to the kind of rule enforcement that gets non-union employers organized. They can also lead to all sorts of lawsuits, all brought before an inhospitable community that is likely to side with the employee. At the very least, such a policy tends to generate bad feelings among employees who fear that one slip might erase years of good service. For that reason you should never surrender your right to make a reasoned judgment and consider the facts before you when making a decision.

Other Factors to Consider

Once you have reviewed where you stand with the rules (or obvious misconduct in the absence of a rule) and the procedure, take another moment to determine whether or not you have disciplined other employees for the same offense and, if so, the nature of the discipline imposed. Was the discipline greater or lesser than what you are considering in this case? What was the reasoning behind the level of discipline imposed in the previous case? When you watch how a professional golfer prepares to make a critical putt on a difficult green, note how he examines the lie from several angles, not just one. Remember, though, that it is seldom necessary to be in lockstep with prior discipline because circumstances are seldom exactly the same.

Distinctions may be called for on the basis of such things as prior good service, seniority, honest mistakes, provocations (where a fight was involved or intemperate words were used), and family problems. If you make distinctions, make note of the distinction at the time you decide on the appropriate discipline. Once this is done, prior discipline, whether greater or lesser, may not be a factor. It is necessary, however, when deviating from discipline from a prior similar offense to distinguish the prior case from the present case as part of the decision-making process. You will then be prepared to explain away any differences if need be. However, if there are no significant distinctions between the current problem and past discipline, you should be concerned about the possibility of a claim of discrimination by reason of disparate treatment.

If you are in doubt about the appropriate penalty or even the guilt of the employee, but circumstances are such that you do not want the employee on the premises, by all means suspend her "pending investigation" or "pending decision." Make the suspension for the period of time you think will be necessary to complete your investigation or whatever else needs to be done, but do not allow matters to drag out. If you find that the employee should not have been suspended in the first place, do the right thing and pay her for the time lost.

If in the past you have been too lenient and a particular problem such as absenteeism has persisted, you can tighten a rule by giving clear notice to all employees of the new, more rigorous standard. This is best done in writing, with the notice widely published and distributed to employees by handout and posting on the bulletin board. When enforcing this new standard, remind employees that the rules are stricter and that former, more lenient policies no longer apply.

It may be a good idea to have a break-in period for some new rules, where for a specified period of time the old disciplinary level is continued or only slightly increased, to accustom employees to the new standard. Any offenses taking place in the transition period should be subject to both limited discipline as well as a reminder of the penalty to be imposed by the stricter rule.

The remaining steps in the decision-making process are designed to help you reach an appropriate level of discipline. As always in these circumstances, if there is doubt as to the correctness of your contemplated decision, this is the time to seek the advice of an experienced employment lawyer.

You should also follow established policies and procedures when issuing discipline. Consider this scenario: The employer operates a chain of fast-food restaurants, and a new employee working at the cash register claims she has been sexually harassed by her supervisor. The employer reprimands the supervisor and transfers the complaining employee to a new location. Does this resolve the sexual harassment claim? Perhaps, if the employee does not claim that the transfer was a substantial inconvenience or if it does not cause her to quit because of distance or some other relevant factor.

Suppose at the new location the supervisor is, by policy, required to check out cash drawers in the presence of the employee. One night, though, the supervisor says, "Go ahead and clock out, it's not necessary for you to stay," and sends the employee away. The next day, the supervisor accuses the employee of being substantially short of cash and fires her. By not following the established protocol, the supervisor has just created a very strong claim of retaliation because the employee had previously made a complaint of sexual harassment. In short, the employee's attorney could make a strong showing that the employer must have considered the employee undesirable because soon after her complaint, she was transferred and then set up for a pretextual discharge claiming that she was either grossly negligent or a thief in circumstances where she had no chance to defend herself. If a court or jury believes the employee when she denies any theft or error—and they probably will—the employer is going to lose that case!

Employer's Legal Pad—Chapter Nine Checklist

After you've gathered all the facts, all the statements, and all the evidence surrounding an allegation that may lead to an adverse employment action, you can simplify your decision making by answering the ten questions listed at the beginning of this chapter. Here are a few other things to consider before you make a decision:

- Don't allow conflicting statements to prevent you from taking action. Absorb all the points of view, trust your instincts, and then make a decision based on the knowledge you have.

- Use good judgment when compiling disciplinary records. A two-year-old minor infraction should probably not be invoked to support today's major disciplinary action. (But keep all records in the employee's personnel file.)

- Be careful with zero tolerance policies that rob you of the power of good judgment except for the most serious infractions. These policies take discretion away from managers and supervisors.

- Note any important differences between this case and other cases where you have decided on disciplinary measures. In the absence of important distinctions such as seniority, honest mistakes, or provocation, you could face a disparate treatment lawsuit down the road.

CHAPTER TEN

Implementing Your Decision

You've made an informed and fair decision. Now it's time to act on it. Once you have finished your investigation and deliberations, you must focus on the reason or reasons for discharge or discipline. When you confront the employee, you must make those reasons clear without hesitation or equivocation. Just as the professional golfer lines up his putt, you must line up your clearest and best reason or reasons for discharge or discipline. When doing this, it may be best to ignore petty offenses if they would contribute to an impression that you are piling things on the employee unnecessarily, especially when the primary reason for discharge is strong. In that event, simply note instead that the employee did not have a prior good work record.

How many times have clients told me that they did not want to cite the real reason for discipline because it was too harsh, because it was too hard to prove, or because they feared it might create future litigation? There are times when employers simply do not want to quarrel with the employee over the reasons for discipline. However, if you have followed the investigatory steps already recommended, citing the reasons for action should not be an insurmountable problem.

An employer's reluctance to state the true reason often stems from a fear that it will be sued for defamation. Such a fear is often misplaced because employers may have a legal "privilege" protecting them from a defamation suit when they tell the employee the reason for discharge or other action. Legal privilege, however, will not shield an employer if there are internal communications to other employees, managers, and supervisors who have no need to know the reason for discharge in the event the employee claims that the accusations are false. Once again, a premium is placed on making a careful investigation of the facts. No employer should publicize the reasons for employment action beyond advising those persons who have a need to know for legitimate business reasons.

Perhaps you fear that a defamation action cannot be overcome or you are concerned that some legal assault will be made based on an allegation that the company published untrue facts. In such a case, the employee involved and other persons in the line of communication may be told, "It is our opinion, based upon the facts as we believe them to be, that. . . ." Through such a statement, you have to defend only your opinion and not the ultimate fact. But once again, it must be said that in litigation you will be trying to prove the fact that your opinion was correct. A failure to state the true reasons for your decision and action may have unfortunate consequences; therefore, it is always better to zero in on the real issue and not be diverted by concerns that may never arise.

Direct Evidence (or the Lack Thereof)

Plaintiffs' attorneys can seldom provide direct evidence of unlawful motivation on the part of the employer. This inability compels plaintiffs' attorneys to resort to three forms of indirect evidence. The first two (the preferences of most plaintiffs' attorneys) are disparate treatment and adverse impact. The third form is related to the disparate treatment theory and alleges that the reasons given for discharge are but a pretext designed to conceal the true motive, which is an act of unlawful discrimination. In all cases, the plaintiff's attorney will do all that he can to claim or show that the employer was unfair in the treatment of his client.

Pretext is shown by demonstrating that the reason given for the adverse action was premised on false facts or assumptions. Plaintiffs do not have to show pretext beyond all doubt; they must only provide enough evidence to call into question the employer's reasons for action. Such a showing allows a plaintiff to argue that the reason for discipline was something other than the reason given by the employer. This ultimately allows the jury or fact-finder to infer that the real reason was discriminatory—*if* they believe the plaintiff's claim.

One way a plaintiff's lawyer can make a pretext argument before a jury is by showing that the employer did not disclose the reason for its decision until after a discrimination charge was filed, or that the reason for discharge shifted or changed between the time of discharge and the filing of the charge. This enables the plaintiff's lawyer to argue that the employer's reasons are belated and an afterthought created to try to justify an unlawful discharge. In all likelihood, the judge will let the jury decide whether the employer's reasons were real or a pretext, which places a huge burden upon the employer and its trial counsel. All of this may be avoided by being up front with the employee at all times.

Being Honest with Employees

If you cannot tell the employee your reason for action in a direct, plain, and unvarnished manner, that is a sign that something is wrong and must be fixed before you take a final step and implement your decision. This places a premium on having all the facts at your command and, if any assumption has been made, that you are satisfied that it was correct.* This makes it difficult, if not impossible, for the plaintiff to discredit the employer's reason for taking action.

Imagine a scenario in which an employer has been sued for age discrimination for terminating a longtime salesperson on the basis of poor performance. The salesperson received no counseling or corrective action and was not told the real reason in an outright manner when he was let go. The plaintiff's attorney might question the employer along the following lines:

Attorney: You have stated that you terminated Mr. Anderson because he was not producing a satisfactory level of sales in his territory.

Employer: That is correct.

Attorney: Mr. Anderson testified that he was fifty-six years old. Do you dispute his age claim?

Employer: No.

Attorney: Who replaced Mr. Anderson?

Employer: Tom Jones.

Attorney: How old was Mr. Jones?

Employer: Twenty-seven.

Attorney: Mr. Anderson said he worked for the company for thirty-four years. Is that correct?

Employer: Yes.

Attorney: Did you ever speak to Mr. Anderson about his failure to meet his sales quotas?

---

*An employer may make an honest mistake and not be guilty of employment discrimination; however, the employer has the burden of satisfying a jury that there was an "honest mistake."

Employer: We had a sales meeting where we urged employees to meet or exceed their sales quotas and showed the results of their efforts.

Attorney: Perhaps you misunderstood my question. I want the court and jury to know whether or not you had a specific meeting with Mr. Anderson and told him the level of his sales was unsatisfactory.

Employer: Not as such, but he should have known he was not meeting his quotas.

Attorney: Did you ever meet with Mr. Anderson to determine why his sales did not meet the quotas you set?

Employer: No.

Attorney: Did you ever travel with Mr. Anderson to see what, if anything, he was doing wrong?

Employer: No.

Attorney: Did you ever audit his expense accounts and sales reports to see if he was making the sales calls he reported?

Employer: No.

Attorney: As far as you knew, he was making a real effort to meet your business expectations?

Employer: He was not getting the job done.

Attorney: Perhaps you misunderstood my question. You have no reason to believe that Mr. Anderson was not making every effort to meet your sales quota, do you?

Employer: No.

Attorney: When you terminated Mr. Anderson after thirty-four years of employment, did you tell him why he was being let go?

Employer: I told him his termination was part of a company reorganization and realignment.

Attorney: So you did not tell him he was let go because of not meeting sales expectations?

Employer: No.

Attorney: Mr. Anderson had no warning that he might lose his job because of his level of sales, did he?

Employer: He should have known that layoff was a possibility.

Attorney: How would he know he might lose his job when you never criticized his work?

As you can see, the employer would have no good answer to this question. Even if there was a great disparity in sales between the plaintiff and other salespeople, a court would probably permit a jury to determine whether or not there was pretext involved simply because there were no warnings given and the real reason for termination was never discussed. Read on to see just how lame the employer's reasoning can be:

Attorney: How does Tom Jones's sales compare with Mr. Anderson's in the year before he was terminated?

Employer: As I told Mr. Anderson, there was reorganization and realignment of sales territories. We cannot compare the sales of the two because of geographic changes.

Attorney: What was Mr. Anderson's territory?

Employer: The states of Illinois, Iowa, Minnesota, and North and South Dakota.

Attorney: What is Mr. Jones's territory?

Employer: Illinois, Iowa, and Minnesota.

Attorney: What happened to the North and South Dakota territories?

Employer: Oh! That has been assigned to John Smith.

Attorney: Let's sum up the facts: An older, long-service employee has been terminated and replaced with a younger person with far less service with the company?

Employer: That's true.

Attorney: You say his poor sales were a cause of his termination but he was never warned and never told the real reason for his dismissal?

Employer: Yes, but only because I did not want to aggravate Mr. Anderson.

Attorney: At this time you do not know whether the replacement is doing a better job or a worse job than Mr. Anderson?

Employer: We think it's better.

Attorney: But you have no sales figures to prove that, do you?

Employer: No.

Attorney: Why did you reduce the sales territory?

Employer: To ensure better sales coverage.

Attorney: Why didn't you let Mr. Anderson work the reduced territory before you decided to terminate him?

Employer: We did not think it would make a difference.

This age discrimination case is headed for the jury, which will no doubt find in favor of the employee. Here is a longtime employee who was not given a warning of poor performance, was not monitored to see if he was actually performing his job, was not worked with to improve his performance, and was replaced, in part, by a much younger employee. To add insult to injury, the size of the sales territory was reduced and the plaintiff was never given a chance to prove his worth in a smaller territory.

Contrast this situation with one in which a discharged employee meets with his lawyer and asks her to bring a discrimination case against his former employer.

Lawyer: What were you told was the reason for your discharge?

Employee: That my sales were too low.

Lawyer: Were you given any advance warning that your sales were insufficient?

Employee: A couple of times.

Lawyer: What were you told?

Employee: At my last annual review, they said my sales were 40 percent below budget. And they said something similar the year before.

Lawyer: Was that true?

Employee: Yes, but my territory was too large to cover and I told them so.

Lawyer: What was their reply to that excuse?

Employee: They offered to reduce my territory or to give me an assistant to make sales calls on smaller customers, but I did not want my opportunities reduced and I did not want to train someone whom they might use to replace me, so I told them no.

At this point the potential plaintiff's lawyer knows she has a problem that must be overcome if she is to prevail because she can anticipate the employer's defense. If the discharged salesperson's replacement has met or exceeded the amount anticipated by the employer, the discharged employee will have a hard time getting his case before a jury and may well find himself out of court well before trial.

Always give employees fair warning when possible and the fact-based reason for termination. The reason for this is that in most cases where an employee brings suit, there is no direct evidence of discrimination. This means that the court will rely on a shifting burden of proof requiring the employee to prove a minimal entitlement to sue and, in turn, requiring the employer to prove a valid, nondiscriminatory reason for discipline. Once that has been done, the employee must be able to successfully call into question whether the employer's reasons were false or he will lose his case, often before trial. The decision-making stage is vital and you should then implement your decision without artful maneuvering to go around a perceived problem. If there is a problem, deal with it!

Once you have made your decision and you are ready to act, confront the employee, preferably in person and with a witness. Be prepared to deal with the employee's objections, especially accusing questions such as, "You didn't fire so-and-so for this." Be alert for employee comments about facts you have not considered. This should not happen if you have properly questioned the employee before making your decision, but if it does, then the employee should be asked why he did not mention these facts before.

Sometimes the employee wants the reason for his discharge in writing. Sometimes employees are furnished a written statement of the reason for discharge. In my home state of Missouri, in certain circumstances, the law requires a "letter of dismissal" truthfully stating the nature and character of the employee's service and the "true cause of dismissal."* Failure to furnish such a letter can get you sued. If the

---

*State laws vary from state to state; therefore, any written communication from a disciplined employee should be a "red light" warning to check and see if it creates any legal obligation on your part.

cause for dismissal can be discredited, you can be sued for not stating the true reason for discharge. There is nothing wrong with furnishing the employee with a written statement explaining the reason for discipline or discharge if you have done everything right. If you do not give the employee reasons for your action in writing the employees file should document the reason for any personnel action taken.

One final note: Do nothing to hinder the discharged employee in the search for a new job. Not only will you avoid a retaliatory action, but to the extent he has earnings, they will offset any potential claim for damages. This does not mean that you should make an untrue recommendation in his behalf.

Employer's Legal Pad—Chapter Ten Checklist

When you confront an employee to announce any kind of adverse action, be sure to explain the reasons for the action clearly and unequivocally. Be honest and straightforward, even if it's uncomfortable. Remember, it will only be more uncomfortable if you end up saying it from the witness stand. If the action you're about to take is fair, communicating the reasons directly will reduce the odds of a lawsuit.

- Avoid claims of pretext by documenting your decision. (If you fire someone in a protected class for, say, violating the attendance policy, be sure to have a copy of that person's attendance record.)

- Discuss the reasons behind an adverse action with others only on a need-to-know basis when the reason for the discharge might be alleged to be defamatory.

- Know your state and local laws surrounding the termination of an employee.

Paperwork and Reality

Throughout this book I have emphasized the need to document every event. Many routine things are documented as a matter of course. Common plant documents such as employee evaluations may already exist. They may help you, but they may also hurt you. You need to take care with all sorts of paperwork, such as evaluations and disciplinary reports.

Employee Evaluations

Evaluations based on objective factors are good as long as the employer's actions based on those evaluations are fair and equal. Evaluations and actions that are subjective in nature, in whole or in part, may create problems. This is not to say that subjective judgments are bad or illegal, sometimes they are necessary, but they do require care in the making.

Virtually every employment defense lawyer has had to tell a client that she should not take the disciplinary action contemplated because it would be inconsistent with a previous favorable employee evaluation. Evaluations are usually completed by first-line supervisors and, as often as not, are never scrutinized at the next level up the chain of command but given only cursory review, if any. Supervisors do not like to offend those working for them by being a tough grader of performance. Frankly, I would rather have no review than an unrealistic review when defending a case. For that reason, the work of the reviewer should be scrutinized and, when necessary, revised before the review is discussed with the employee.

All too often subjective evaluation forms are couched in terms of "excellent," "good," and "fair." These are general terms that lack a truly objective meaning. In addition, negative terms are often omitted or minimized. This type of employee evaluation is sometimes called "olive grading," because even a small olive is graded "large" and the bigger the olive, the more superlative the adjective. For the employer to evaluate an employee accurately, there must either be a written essay on the employee's performance or an evaluation system that truly reflects employee performance.

I do not claim to be a human resources professional, but in the absence of a better format, I suggest a review system that evaluates employees in the following terms:

- Consistently below average
- Occasionally below average
- Average (alternatively, you could say "good" for your middle ranking)
- Occasionally above average
- Consistently above average

While this does not quantify the employee's performance precisely, it may be more specific in terms of situating the employee in relation to her peers. In addition, it might focus the supervisor's attention on a real standard of performance and thereby avoid the use of "good," "excellent," and other general words that may be too generously applied where there is no real context for evaluating "good." "Average" may be too general a term, but I use it to avoid being overly positive or negative in hopes that the evaluator does not lavish undeserved praise on the unworthy. After all, that praise may be used against the employer at a later date.

While we are rethinking the review procedure, do not forget to look at the evaluation form itself for glitches or other possible problems. In one recent case, a clerical employee, Sally, as part of her job summarized the attendance facts including dates of absence and tardiness for another employee, Gene, on the company's evaluation form. Sally forwarded the form to the appropriate supervisor, Jeff, so he could complete Gene's performance evaluation and give him a grade. Gene's attendance record for the previous twelve months was very good at the time Sally summarized his attendance. Unfortunately, by the time Jeff reviewed Gene a full month later, Gene had started to accrue what later became an excessive number of unexcused absences, the second of which came the very day (but after) Jeff signed the evaluation form. Jeff rated Gene's attendance as "excellent" based on the outdated information on the form. A short time later, Jeff realized that Gene had incurred a third unexcused absence in a matter of five or six weeks. Jeff issued a warning to Gene threatening future discipline if his attendance did not improve, all the while failing to recall or refer to his previous unexplained conclusion that Gene's attendance was "excellent."

Gene was later fired after accumulating several warnings and a suspension for various acts of misconduct. Gene alleged that his discharge was discriminatory for several reasons. When litigation began, Gene held up the "excellent" attendance evaluation and compared it with the warning received only six weeks later for poor attendance as proof that the employer was unjustly papering his personnel file in an effort to create a reason for discharge. The failure of the form to specify the attendance period covered and Jeff's delay in signing the form stunned both Sally and Jeff at their depositions because they could not readily reconcile the inconsistency between the "excellent" rating and the subsequent warning issued to Gene for poor attendance. If the form had stated that it was documenting the employee's attendance record for a specific span of time , there would have been no need to explain the month-long gap between Sally's work and Jeff's evaluation, during which Gene's excessive absences began. Had Jeff completed the evaluation promptly upon receipt of the form, the problem would also have been prevented. Last, had Jeff explained the apparent contradiction when he drafted the warning, the problem would not have arisen.

Avoiding Haste in Completing Paperwork

Sometimes we can be too hasty in completing paperwork. I once had such a case before the enactment of the Americans with Disabilities Act (ADA). A probationary employee suffered a ruptured eardrum, purportedly because of loud noises on the production floor. The treating physician determined that the employee must work in quieter surroundings. The company had no such work and summarily terminated the employee without the benefit of a gentle letdown. The employee claimed that she had been the victim of discrimination because she had sustained a workers compensation injury.

The employee sued and won a verdict. Had the employer not been in such haste to issue a discharge notice, the employee could not have claimed discrimination. What the employer should have done was call the employee into the office, review available jobs with her, and reach a determination with her as to whether there was an open job she could perform or that no such job existed, thereby paving the way to terminate her employment. Such a procedure will also stand you in good stead in any ADA case.

Writing the Disciplinary Report

When writing the disciplinary report, state the nature of the discipline being imposed and the reason(s) for it. There is no need to recapitulate all of the facts of the offense if they are properly documented elsewhere, but you should at a minimum state the ultimate facts in a brief statement. For example, you could write one of the following things:

- You have been absent (or tardy) on seven occasions in the past sixty days: May 8, 10, 15, and 21; June 4, 5, and 12.

- You were observed clocking out for _____ [name the employee].

- You started a fight with _____ [name the employee], who had done nothing to provoke this kind of violence.

- A search of your locker resulted in the discovery of a half empty 750-milligram bottle of gin.

Note that the first example sets forth the dates of the attendance problems. This is important in order to discourage a dispute over dates at some later time. In the second example, you should name the beneficiary of the misconduct because he is also a party and should be disciplined for his complicity. In the third example, there is a pardoning of the other employee in the fray. (If the other employee was provocative, that act might be insufficient to justify an assault; on the other hand, such an act might ameliorate the seriousness of the offense.) The last example is a simple statement of the operative fact.

Identify by name or number any specific rules that have been broken. Do not necessarily tell the employee everything you know. Some facts, and perhaps all facts, should have been disclosed when the employee was asked to explain his conduct, so there is no need to restate them all here. The important thing is that you have the facts already committed to writing, including the employee's defenses.

The disciplinary report should be dated and signed by the decision maker or makers. Do not prepare a report to be issued by someone else who is not involved in the matter but is merely in the chain of command; his participation in any defense is worthless and confusing. There is an exception to this last caveat: If you have a system in which a timekeeper sends a report to a supervisor when attendance problems indicate the need for discipline (as is common in a no-fault attendance program), it is appropriate to notify the supervisor of the need to take action because she may not be keeping track of attendance. If the latter is the case, make certain the supervisor follows through with issuing the report.

The employee should be encouraged to sign the disciplinary report. If he refuses, then that should be noted on the form to reflect the employee's intransigence. The employee should receive a copy of the disciplinary report and, where applicable, a copy should be forwarded to any union concerned.

Employer's Legal Pad—Chapter Eleven Checklist

Evaluations can help or hurt an employer. It's important for all managers and supervisors to keep employee evaluations objective and honest.

- Consider assigning a third party to review employee evaluations with line managers who write them.

- Review your company's evaluation form for glitches, potential misunderstandings, or contradictions.

- When giving a poor evaluation that leads to discipline, always prepare a brief, written disciplinary report stating relevant facts, dates, and people instead of relying upon the evaluation form alone.

CHAPTER TWELVE

Unemployment Compensation Claims

The primary reason to focus on the true reason for discharge or layoff and to accurately communicate that reason to the employee is to discourage her from claiming that she was given multiple—perhaps even inconsistent—reasons for her dismissal. One of the first opportunities an employer has to avoid this mistake is in responding to claims for unemployment compensation.

Providing the Necessary Information

Mistakes are often made when an employer is providing information to a deputy of the local office of the state division of employment security concerning the reason(s) for an employee's departure. This information is provided in writing by completing a form or by answering the deputy's questions over the telephone. The mistake may also be made or compounded when attending the unemployment hearing.

Do not leave preparation and planning for one of these hearings to an untutored supervisor or manager. Hire an attorney (especially if you anticipate future legal problems) or designate one person to serve as your company's primary representative. Over time, this representative will develop a measure of expertise and may consult the company attorney only from time to time for any necessary advice.

If you have done your job correctly, you will give the state agency the real reason for the claimant's lack of employment in simple and concise terms. If the claimant does not agree with your assessment, then a hearing may be conducted in person or by telephone during which the agency will attempt to resolve any factual issues. If there is no factual dispute, it does not mean that you will prevail in opposing the claim. The agency may determine that your reasons were not sufficient under state law to deny the employee compensation. An example of this would be the case of an employee laid off because he could not do the work even though he tried his best.

Claimants are usually not represented by an attorney at these hearings, but at some later point a plaintiff's attorney may rely on the record made at the hearing or the agency's ultimate decision to prove that you discriminated against her client. It is therefore important to develop a good record consistent with the facts surrounding separation at the hearing.

You may be able to secure a copy of the transcript or the tape recording of the hearing from the agency for minimal expense. Most state agencies maintain these records for only a limited period of time; therefore, it is strongly recommended that you request the record of the proceeding any time there is a real probability that the matter is headed toward another trial or judicial resolution. Bear in mind that a lawsuit may not be filed until many months or years after the discharge. If you wait for an action to be filed, it may be too late to secure the record.

If you intend to represent your company yourself at the unemployment hearing (rather than have your attorney do so), then you must prepare for a mini-trial at which you will have the burden of proof. Assemble all the documentary evidence and other physical evidence you have and be prepared to submit a copy (not the original) to the agency or at least show it at the hearing if it is not subject to ready duplication.

Hearsay Testimony

Hearsay testimony is testimony by a witness about what others have said rather than what the witness himself said. Hearsay is generally allowed by the hearing officer or agency but is not afforded the same consideration as direct, firsthand testimony, so you will need a firsthand witness to the essential facts at the hearing.

There are many exceptions to the hearsay rule, but there are two that you should know: (1) admissions against interest and (2) business records. The first states that what the errant employee has said or written is an acknowledgment of fault and/or an admission that works against his interests in some manner may be used against the employee. If the employee has admitted part or all of his wrongdoing in writing, that document is very powerful evidence on which you may rely. Oral statements are also admissible. The exception regarding business records (such as policies, rules, time cards, attendance reports, past disciplinary reports, medical excuse slips, and doctor's reports) states that such documents are usually admissible if someone can attest to the fact that they were maintained in the normal course of business and are true and correct to the best of the witness's knowledge. Statements of witnesses gathered during the investigative stage are also usually admissible but they are hearsay and will not serve to overcome the former employee's direct testimony; for that reason you should have at least one witness with firsthand knowledge of the facts testify.

Testifying at the Hearing

You will be asked to state your reasons for dismissing the employee and to present your testimonial and documentary evidence. Because hearings are usually scheduled for a very short period of time, frequently only thirty to forty-five minutes, prepare to go straight to the ultimate issue. You usually have the opportunity to say, "We fired John Doe because. . . ." The hearing officer will ask you (or your witness) to state facts that you should present in a simple but organized fashion. Approaching the issue chronologically works where the record is accrued over a period of time. If, however, a single event caused the discharge, that event may be a starting point for your presentation. Keep in mind that the only issue to be decided at the unemployment hearing is whether the reason the claimant is unemployed allows him to receive benefits from the state.

The hearing officer may then ask questions about your direct evidence. The claimant is permitted to cross-examine each witness. Claimant questions are often poorly phrased and disorganized, so listen to the question and respond with a statement of the relevant facts. This is where knowing the discharged employee's excuse(s) really pays off because you can anticipate his questions and be prepared to answer them. Your answers should go directly to the questions asked and not stray into irrelevant matters. If you believe that something more should be said, you will have a chance to ask further questions or make statements after being cross-examined. If the hearing examiner omits this opportunity, speak up and state that you have something more to add.

Do not let your answers degenerate into an argument with a former employee. You can usually avoid this problem by keeping to the facts, even if your answer is a simple statement that the information posed by the cross-question is not true. If the discharged employee tries to argue with you, point out that fact to the hearing examiner and ask for a ruling.

After you have presented your case and have been cross-examined, the discharged employee must present his case. If he abandons the excuse he presented when he was given his due process hearing, you will have a chance to ask him questions on cross-examination about why he changed his story.

You or your representative will also have an opportunity to confront the discharged employee with his admissions and any other facts you think the employee may admit. Ask simple, straightforward questions such as "You told me the reason you clocked out employee Smith was . . . ?" or "You did not give us a doctor's note for your absence on July 31, did you?" Do not begin with a long recitation of facts you believe or hope to be true and finish with a preconceived conclusion. In addition, do not waste time with undisputed facts that are already a matter of record or by asking questions that involve facts your witnesses have testified about but the claimant has not denied. If the claimant is asked about facts that are already a matter of record, he may deny those facts and raise a factual issue. On the other hand, if he fails or forgets to deny those facts, they will be uncontested and that will be to your benefit.

On rebuttal, you will have an opportunity to present witnesses to refute anything new brought up by the claimant (provided your witnesses can testify firsthand about any facts known to them). Endeavor to place every relevant fact into the record either by testimony or by document. If the hearing officer refuses to allow this evidence, at least you will have a record of your offer. Make certain the record reflects just what you are offering and why it is relevant. Keep a record of every document put in evidence by both sides, including any identifying number or letter used by the hearing officer. After you have done your job, the issue is now in other hands and you must await the result.

For your benefit, I will pass along my visceral instinct after years of observing unemployment hearings: If the state has a lot of money in the unemployment kitty it will tend to be generous; if times are bad and money is scarce it is amazing how parsimonious the state can be.

You may choose not to contest a claim for benefits if you believe the employee will be content with unemployment benefits and leave it at that. You should avoid this mistake because the employee may claim he was discriminated against in his claim or otherwise treated unfairly and if there is a subsequent lawsuit his attorney will pettifog your failure to contest the claim as an admission against interest on your part. On the other hand, you may strike a bargain with the employee to the effect that you will not contest his claim for benefits if he resigns. In that event, the agreement should be placed in writing and signed by all parties. (The agreement **may** be sufficient to amount to a compromise settlement agreement that will preclude litigation, except in age discrimination cases because the Older Workers Benefit Protection Act [29 U.S.C. §626 (f)] requires specific language to achieve settlement with an employee protected by the Age Discrimination in Employment Act.) The agreement **will** prevent the employee from using the fact that you did not protest the award of benefits against you in some later action.

Employer's Legal Pad—Chapter Twelve Checklist

Many employment-related lawsuits are born when an unemployment compensation claim is denied. At this point, if your reasons for dismissing the employee were vague or inconsistent, they could come back to haunt you.

- Think of an unemployment hearing as a mini-trial where the burden of proof is on the employer.

- Designate one person in your organization to communicate with the state unemployment office and to answer its questions.

- Consider hiring an attorney to represent the company if you expect a discrimination suit by the employee.

- Request a copy of the record of any unemployment insurance hearing. In the event of a lawsuit you may need it, even years later.

CHAPTER THIRTEEN

Problem Employees

All employers have problem employees—those, for example, that abuse alcohol and drugs, are frequently absent, or engage in criminal behavior. In the spirit of avoiding lawsuits before they occur, you may want to review your company's policies regarding drugs and alcohol, attendance, and criminal behavior. Employers with clear, well-distributed policies—and the courage to take prompt, consistent, fair action when these policies are violated—have less chance of getting sued. In the event of a lawsuit, they have a much stronger chance of prevailing.

Alcohol and Drug Use

You should have clear rules on drinking, drug use, and testing. During my early years of practice, while it was commonplace to fire an employee who had a drink on the job, executives often had cocktails during a restaurant lunch. Today's working environment, however, does not often tolerate or accommodate those who drink at lunch. Drinking during the workday results in poor performance and possible injuries to self and others. There is much to be said in favor of having the same rules for all employees (with the exception of after-hours entertaining).

The right to test employees for the use of alcohol or drugs is vital to the defense of any disciplinary action and ensures that any action taken has a foundation in fact. Appendix D contains a sample rule for such testing. The rule provides for discharge for a refusal to cooperate as well as for a possible second chance for those who test positive, accompanied by follow-up testing. There is little incentive for the employee to cooperate in the absence of a second chance. However, you might not want to provide a second chance when the employee is caught using alcohol or drugs during working hours as opposed to a situation where the employee is suspected of such use. Testing is necessary to establish the true facts.

Employees who habitually use alcohol or drugs have generally learned how to impede the employer's investigation. Those with alcohol or drug problems often try to postpone the test as long as possible so that they have a chance to metabolize any substances in their system. The only way to deal with this situation is to have a supervisor take the employee to the testing facility directly and without delay or excuse. If you simply send the employee to the testing facility unaccompanied, he will find a way to delay. Besides, you don't want to be accused of having the employee drive impaired on his way to a test.

The Attendance Problem

Attendance problem patterns often appear on Mondays and Fridays and before holidays. There are also problems with employees who are chronically tardy, who leave early, or who take long lunch hours. The only solution is discipline that either corrects the problem or allows you to fire the offender.

Discipline becomes a problem when different supervisors and managers take independent action. After all, no two people act alike in the same circumstance, and you may have variances within your own house that contribute to discrimination claims. To overcome this problem, many employers have resorted to a no-fault attendance policy that assigns points for leaving early, tardiness, and absence. (An example of such a policy is given in Appendix E.) These policies work only when someone accurately keeps track of attendance, forwards the information to the relevant supervisor for timely action, and that supervisor acts. Actions taken under such programs usually consist of progressive discipline such as warnings, suspensions, and finally, discharge. My personal preference is to avoid programs that allow employees x number of instances of being tardy and y number of absences. A good program counts every attendance violation and assigns greater or lesser weight to a particular offense. A good program also provides a means for an employee to clear his record by good attendance.

Problems arise when employees violate the program faster than they can be disciplined. When that happens, get to the employee as soon as possible and take the strongest possible discipline short of discharge. Make it clear to the employee that her absenteeism outpaced your ability to issue warnings, and should it happen in the future, she will not be given a second chance but will be held strictly accountable under the terms of the program.

The advent of the Family and Medical Leave Act (FMLA) has infringed on the employer's freedom of action if the employer is subject to that law because an absence that must be excused under FMLA cannot be counted as an offense to the attendance program. As a result, great care must be taken in classifying the absence as legally protected or unprotected. In some instances, you will be well advised to tell the employee to apply for leave under FMLA rather than penalize her for an excusable absence or be faulted for not making certain she knows her rights under that law.

In a no-fault attendance system, it sometimes is advantageous to the employer to give the employee a last chance by allowing one more step before the discharge that the policy provides. It is also a good idea to provide the means to accelerate discipline when an employee "games" the system by taking his absences to the brink of discipline and then backing off until he has room for another absence. You can do this by reserving the right to invoke a special review and accelerate discipline when you detect such a pattern. In this instance, make certain the special review contains a warning to the employee that he will be fired should he continue to engage in such a pattern.

Regardless of whether you have a no-fault policy or not, do not hesitate to tell the employee during discipline about any pattern of absences that you have detected. This places you on record early on and makes it more difficult for the employee to have an excuse that works for all of the days in the pattern.

Criminal Behavior

On occasion, an employee is arrested and charged with a crime ranging from drunk driving to something even more serious. From an employer's perspective, if an employee goes to prison, most of the problems disappear. Unless a union contract affords the employee a measure of protection, you may dismiss the employee for attendance reasons. Take advantage of that opportunity. You can almost always rehire the employee if he is exonerated or serves his time and you want him back in the workforce. But if you fail to take action, you may be setting a precedent for the next time an employee is arrested and jailed.

It's an entirely different circumstance if the employee is released on bail pending trial. If there is a union contract and there is no reason to fire the employee for attendance or reporting violations, you should have your attorney examine the facts to determine whether or not the discharge is sustainable in arbitration. If employment is at-will,* then you should see if the charge is sufficiently serious for you to assert that discharge or unpaid suspension pending trial is appropriate. In this respect, give careful consideration to whether or not you are overreacting, to the attitude of the rest of the workforce toward the employee, and to any danger the employee might pose if she were allowed to continue working. If the criminal charge is sufficiently serious and you are contemplating discharge, you must examine your company's overall disciplinary records to see if you will be vulnerable to a claim of disparate impact or disparate treatment because similar criminal charges have been tolerated in the past.

You may question an employee on the facts that led to his arrest. Where possible, asking pertinent questions on guilt or innocence should be part of your decision-making process. The employee has no Fifth Amendment rights to refuse to speak to you about his involvement and defense (although a labor arbitrator might rule differently in a union plant). Moreover, what the employee tells you is not a privileged communication exempt from discovery by the prosecutor.

Most employees facing serious charges will refuse to talk to you on the advice of their attorney. If this happens, you can show that you tried your best to give the employee the benefit of the doubt, citing his refusal to address the issues created by his arrest in defense of your ultimate decision. If you have had problems with the employee in the

---

*"At-will" means that either party may terminate the employment relationship at its discretion. Employment discrimination laws limit the employer's freedom of action in at-will employment relationships.

past or he has little in the way of seniority, all else being equal, the crime for which he was arrested may be serious enough to warrant discharge. You should always be prepared, though, to justify just why you chose discharge instead of some other alternative.

If you do not want the employee back in the workplace but are unsure if you want to fire him, then an indefinite suspension pending trial is an easy way to postpone what could be a difficult decision. One potential problem: The employee may plead to the charge and receive a suspended sentence or probation. If that happens, you can expect the employee to knock at the door asking to be reinstated.

The Dangerous Employee

Employers have been and will continue to be sued for negligent hiring. Assigning a convicted rapist to work with a female employee has resulted in more than one successful lawsuit following an assault. The good intentions that go with giving a convicted felon a second chance are laudable, but those intentions must be tempered with a realistic appraisal of what might go wrong if the employee has not reformed. The employee must indicate a genuine desire to join mainstream society and know that there will be little or no tolerance for misbehavior. With whom and where the employee will work are essential factors to consider.

Another concern is the employee who may lose control and shoot his fellow workers and supervisors. How can you spot such a potential danger? Experts advise you to watch those with uncontrollable tempers, those obsessed with firearms, and other signs of a lack of self-control.* My only experience comes from after-the-fact anecdotes

---

*As a lifelong shooter, collector, and hunter I think this opinion is a "shot in the dark" and is pure guesswork based upon their own concept of political correctness. I have known numerous hunters, competitive shooters, and gun aficionados, none of whom has ever shot anyone despite

from those with some knowledge. In those instances the employee had been fired and entered the premises for post-discharge business purposes. The employee secreted the firearm in a lunch box or a lunch bag and pulled it out and began shooting those he considered to have brought about his discharge. Beware of disgruntled employees bringing anything that might conceal a weapon into a meeting. Secure your premises so that exits and entries are controlled against unwanted invasion. Even though an employee might do some damage, there will still be a measure of warning and control if you exercise care. In addition, from time to time you may learn that an employee has homicidal or suicidal ideas. There are restrictions upon sharing confidential medical information with others, but this should not prohibit advising key personnel to watch the employee for signs of trouble.

The best way to avoid having a violent employee is not to hire one in the first place. Check references, police records, and motor vehicle records. A record of domestic disputes and alcohol and substance abuse as well as any history of violent behavior should serve as a warning sign unless these events are so far in the past as to be of little or no consequence. Try to anticipate situations where tempers may flare up, and do what you can to defuse the situation.

If you anticipate threats or violence, have security (or a large friend) present when you administer discipline. Where possible, administer discipline on a Friday afternoon so that the employee has the weekend to cool down. At the conclusion of any termination interview, have the employee escorted while he gathers his possessions and leaves the premises. If threats are made, notify the police and consider court action such as a restraining order and injunction. Court action

---

any anger they might feel. I personally would be more concerned with the congenitally angry person and the loner who has a dark and secretive side to his personality and/or made threatening comments.

may serve as a wake-up call to the employee (even though it has little meaning to someone who is determined to wreak havoc). Last, hire appropriate security to prevent the dangerous employee from reentering company premises.

The Insubordinate Employee

The insubordinate employee needs to be put in his place fast. There is no reason to tolerate an angry, in-your-face worker who verbally abuses supervisors or management with profane or obscene remarks. Employees may also engage in other overly confrontational acts or conduct that also warrant discipline.

This type of person is essentially a bully whose behavior cannot be permitted to continue unhindered. Any supervisor who falls victim to such an individual should receive immediate support in documenting what has occurred. The employee should be sternly reprimanded after investigation and even fired if the offense was sufficiently serious. If the employee's immediate supervisor is not strong enough to do the job, someone else must step in and handle it. The sooner the errant employee learns who is boss, the better off he and the company will be. If you have a union plant and the insubordinate employee holds union office, he may be vigorous in his union advocacy but he is not entitled to be rude, insubordinate, or profane—and never entitled to make threats of physical violence.

Supervisors may also engage in abusive behavior. Needless to say, bullying by supervisors has no justification, and they cannot be permitted to provoke subordinates or create other legal problems.

The Troublemaker

Unfortunately, troublemakers may have some form of legal protection. A troublemaker's protests may not be subject to discipline if she purports to be protesting some form of illegal discrimination such as race, sex, or religious bias, if she claims there are occupational health and safety violations, or if she is engaging in so-called "protected concerted activities." She may be subject to discipline, however, if she crosses over some line by her conduct, but that crossover point cannot be easily determined in advance. When an employee action purports to be in protest of something the company has allegedly done or failed to do, that is your signal to seek legal advice to determine if there is any likelihood of legally protected activity on the part of the employee.*

Regarding "protected concerted activities," the National Labor Relations Act protects both union and nonunion activities, which includes the "protected activity" of individual employees. Two or more employees acting together in concert with respect to wages, hours, and conditions of employment (and you cannot find a much broader definition than that) are engaged in legally "protected concerted activity" if their actions are reasonable in the circumstances. So if two or more employees confront a manager to complain about almost anything or to request anything, you cannot discipline or discharge them for that unless they engage in some grossly insubordinate act or other clearly unacceptable conduct. For example, a work stoppage or refusal to do a job to protest an unsafe working condition may or may not be protected. The same may be said of one employee purporting to act on behalf of other employees. A competent labor lawyer must examine the employees' actions to determine whether or not a measure of legal protection exists.

If in doubt and you cannot tolerate the troublesome employee's presence in the workplace any longer, suspend the employee pending investigation. Then promptly investigate and seek legal advice. If you

---

*For example, the Sarbanes-Oxley Act provides legal protection against retaliation for whistle-blowers in publicly traded corporations as well as requiring those corporations to establish procedures to accept internal complaints. The Occupational Safety and Health Act provides protection against retaliation for employees reporting purported violations of that act. There may be other such laws, especially at the state level, providing similar protection.

were wrong, you may reinstate the employee with back pay, which is why you should be prompt in following up on the suspension. If the offense warrants discipline, then a suspension or discharge may be appropriate.

The Thief

Anyone who steals or embezzles anything that you attach value to is a thief and should be fired as soon as the relevant facts can be marshaled. (I am not talking about the individual who takes a disposable pen home from the office.) Of course, you should assemble documentation and give the employee due process for your own protection.

You should take precautionary measures to prevent theft and to give employees a means of protecting themselves if they are allowed to take products or materials home. Separating the intake of money from the outflow of money is a good idea where possible. Issuing passes or permission slips to employees who are authorized to remove material is another positive step. Do not tolerate proven theft.

Employer's Legal Pad—Chapter Thirteen Checklist

- It's a good idea to review your company's polices regarding drugs and alcohol. Make sure they cover everyone in the organization and that they're applied fairly and consistently.

- When sending employees for a drug test, consider appointing a supervisor or manager to accompany them. Dispatch them promptly, before any substances are out of their systems.

- Consider a no-fault attendance system that gives points for unexcused absences and tardiness or taking other steps to ensure consistent discipline of attendance problems.

- Understand how FMLA works and when an employee is legally entitled to a leave of absence.

- Do not tolerate insubordinate behavior.

- Consider discharge of employees arrested for felony and major misdemeanor crimes.

- Do background checks of persons you wish to hire.

- Monitor ex-employees who may be hostile if they return to the workplace.

- Be alert for employees who protest over health and safety issues, whether bona fide complaints or not.

- Be alert for two or more employees who raise issues concerning wages, hours, and working conditions.

- Do not tolerate dishonesty at any level.

CHAPTER FOURTEEN

Employees with Special Issues

Employers often must deal with employees who have special issues, such as those who are injured and have workers compensation claims and those with disabilities.

The Accident-Prone and Workers Compensation Claimants

Workers compensation claims are the bane of every employer. Most companies have established protocols for dealing with injured employees, protocols that should be followed. Be aware that a retaliation suit may result if at some later time you have to discipline or discharge an employee who filed a workers compensation claim. The most vulnerable times are within a few months of the injury or while a claim is being litigated.

There are certain fundamental things that you should *not* do to minimize the risk of litigation:

- Do not criticize the employee directly because of her injury or make remarks to others about the injury unless criticism is warranted because of some safety violation.

- If a safety violation is involved, do not make gratuitous comments. Confine the investigation and discipline to events related to the violation.

- Do not complain to the employee about his recovery time; leave that issue to the medical provider. If there is a problem, discuss the matter with the attending physician or find a contrary medical opinion. Do not complain to the employee.

- Do not discuss the claim with the employee or her opposing attorney and that includes comments about the attorney.

- Do not refer to the cost of medical treatment when communicating with the employee.

- Do not be too eager when offering monetary incentives to supervisors and managers to minimize workers compensation claims. Exercise great care here because the overzealous pursuit of that incentive may provide evidence of intent to discriminate.

- When workers compensation costs are totaled up for management review, do not send the injured employee's manager a separate written report of costs. Instead, if possible, bury the costs in some miscellaneous item as opposed to separating them out. If you do have separate reports on the costs of medical treatment and/or settlement costs, the plaintiff's attorney will seek to discover that information. If he gets that information he might browbeat some manager with the numbers, accusing him of firing workers to improve his financials or increase any bonus money based upon profitability. You may raise the cost issue with supervisors and managers discreetly, but if the numbers are reported separately, then the plaintiff can show that you made a major issue of costs and can attempt to infer that firing the plaintiff was a cost-containment action.

If the employee violated safety rules and brought about his own injury, discipline may be appropriate for the safety infraction as opposed to the injury. The only part the injury should play in the disciplinary process is the extent to which it demonstrates the seriousness of the rule violation, not to the fact of injury itself. If you have a workforce that is large enough and you have confidence in your employees, it does no harm to have a safety committee to investigate accidents and determine if rule violations occurred. Such a committee determination would take some of the disciplinary onus from management's shoulders, specifically over issues of guilt or responsibility, although management should always determine the appropriate level of discipline. The use of such a committee also is of value when an employee's safety rule violation injured not himself but another employee.

Drug and alcohol testing is appropriate after an accident because in some states, the employee is penalized monetarily if there is a positive test. A positive test also provides a nondiscriminatory reason for issuing appropriate discipline.

A competent plaintiff's attorney will seek, in discovery, the names of other employees who have sustained injuries leading to substantial medical bills and workers compensation claims, whether or not the individuals continue to be employed or how long they were employed after the injury and/or claim. Once again, the vital nature of good record-keeping is apparent here. There is always some degree of employee turnover, and you can use your business records to show that other employees who sustained injury quit voluntarily or were fired for good and sufficient cause unrelated to their injury. Such records negate the plaintiff's attorney's plan of attack because she then faces problems when trying to premise her client's discrimination claim on action taken against another employee in the past. In addition, when mounting your defense, you may be able to show with your business records that some employees who sustained workers compensation injuries are still employed despite having had more than one injury or having received a large settlement following a substantial injury.

By not making poorly conceived comments about an employee's injury to anyone other than those with a need to know, you deprive the employee of evidence he might use to make a case of discrimination. In the absence of some adverse remark that might be deemed an admission or proof of an intent to discriminate, the employee has only two facts in his favor: (1) the injury, and (2) his dismissal. Unless these two events are so close in time that it raises an inference of discrimination, the employee will not have much of a case. If the employee's lack of proof can be coupled with clear misconduct occurring between his injury and his dismissal, then the employer will have a substantial defense.

Clearly, the facts and circumstances surrounding each accident or injury must be documented. Your insurance carrier has probably given you forms for this purpose and/or assisted you in the creation of a paper trail.

If an employee either fails to report a physical problem or does not attribute a problem to her work, does it mean that you are protected from a future claim? Not necessarily. For example, say an employee believes and even reports to you that her injury was unrelated to her work, but she later claims that she went to a physician and was told that her injury was due to repetitive movement or some other work-related cause. At that time you are deprived of the ability to rely upon her disclaimer of a work-related injury. You are certainly free to contest her claim based on what she said or failed to say after she sustained the injury. But you can't take it for granted that the state workers compensation commission will find the injury noncompensable merely because of her previous opinion or failure to report the injury.

You especially cannot rely on the employee's failure to report the injury or her verbal denial that the injury is work-related in circumstances where you are about to fire her. Suppose the employee is fired for absenteeism related to an injury that neither she nor you believe was caused by her work. Later, the discharged employee consults a doctor (or more likely an attorney who finds a doctor) who attributes part or all of the injury to her work. Not only will she file a claim for compensation but you will be sued for retaliating against her by reason of her lost employment due to industrial injury.* The employee's previous denials of any work-related injury go for naught because she will claim those remarks were made in ignorance of her medical condition. Therefore, it's better not to rely on absences resulting from injury when determining whether or not to discharge an employee unless it's clear that the injury is not work-related.

The Disabled Employee

The Americans with Disabilities Act (ADA) defines "individuals with disabilities" as individuals who have a physical or mental impairment that substantially limits one or more major life activities. The ADA

---

*The employer may also run afoul of the Family and Medical Leave Act and the Americans with Disabilities Act under certain circumstances.

also protects those who have a record of impairment. (These terms can be difficult to interpret and there are over seven hundred U.S. District Courts. That diversity has resulted in different decisions on what are essentially the same set of facts by different courts, all of which make it difficult for good lawyers, let alone lay persons, to be definitive about conditions that qualify for ADA protection.) This broad, if not sloppy, definition is grist in the mill of lawyers. For example, one federal court found that reproduction is a major life activity and provided the employee protection under the ADA. Reproductive ability might be relevant if you are a stallion applying for a job on a Kentucky horse farm but has nothing to do with any job I can think of and in the minds of most is totally irrelevant. However, different rules apply to the employer. In order to exclude people with certain disabilities from a position, the law requires an employer to show a rational relationship between the employment activity required by the job and the employee's disability that renders the person unacceptable as an employee in that particular job.

The employee must be able to perform the essential functions of a job, with or without "reasonable accommodation" (an ambiguous term that has and will generate much litigation). While there have been interpretations of the ADA that require a job offer before an applicant has taken a physical examination, most problems arise after the employee has worked in the business for a period of time. In cases involving both applicants and those already employed, the same burden is placed upon the employer: to investigate whether or not employment is possible with reasonable accommodation of the disabled employee. Reasonable accommodation in theory does not require the employer to go to unreasonable expense, nor does it require the bypassing of the rights and privileges of other employees, including seniority.

Regardless of how obvious it may be to you that no reasonable accommodation can be made in the case of a particular employee, it is usually a good idea to sit down with the employee and ask him how he thinks he could be accommodated so he can perform the essential functions of his job (or possibly other jobs if that is an option). Once again, if you can get his opinion in writing you can remove any future controversy about just what his opinion was at the time. Any failure to consult with the employee will be used against your company in any legal action brought by the employee. Evaluate that opinion against your own judgment to determine if the accommodation would be reasonable or not. As always, if in doubt, consult your attorney for an opinion on the question of reasonable accommodation. Finally, if accommodation is not possible, advise the employee of the reasons why this cannot be done.

Also consult a competent attorney to determine whether or not the employee qualifies for legal protection as a person with a disability, is "perceived or regarded" to be disabled, or has a record of disability. In all three instances, the employee is accorded legal protection. The existence of a legal disability requires a detailed factual inquiry and legal research as to whether or not a court would consider the person disabled. Do not jump to any rash conclusions on your own about what constitutes a disability. Many things you might think of as disabilities have not met that definition as a matter of law in certain instances (for example, morbid obesity, asthma, epilepsy, and temporary ailments), but you should not assume that these exclusions apply in all instances to all employers. These are complicated decisions that require legal input. Furthermore, in the United States there are more than seven hundred federal judges at the district court level, plus twelve federal circuit courts, not to mention state courts. These various courts may reach different conclusions about the same physical or mental conditions on any given set of facts according to their own judgment. Unless a disability is obvious beyond all doubt, do not attempt to make this legal judgment yourself. As for the issue of perception of disability status, the evidence you will face will be based on the verbal and written statements and other actions of managers and supervisors that may be used by a plaintiff-employee to imply that you considered him disabled. This will afford him protection under the law even if he does not in fact meet the definition of disabled.

Be mindful of what you say and do and never acknowledge that an employee is disabled. Stick to the facts: "Employee Jones cannot do this job because he cannot do (this) or (that)." Finally, do not tolerate other employees making fun of or joking about a health problem or physical characteristic because that may give rise to the "perceived or regarded as" concept. In addition to being rude and offensive to the employee, it may be offensive to other employees and it might also give rise to a claim of illegal harassment because of the disability.

Employer's Legal Pad—Chapter Fourteen Checklist

For employees who are not disciplinary problems but who have issues (such as medical conditions) that send up "lawsuit warning flags," be sure to follow your company's established protocols regarding workers compensation claims.

- Understand what you may and may not ask regarding an employee's or applicant's medical condition. If you're in doubt, consult an attorney.

- Know what you may and may not communicate regarding an employee's workers compensation claim.

- While you have a legitimate need to know when to expect an employee to return to work after a work-related injury, do not criticize recovery time—that is an issue for medical providers.

- Do not reference costs of a particular workers compensation claim to the employee or his fellow workers.

- Regardless of how obvious it is to you that no reasonable accommodation can be made to a person who is or may be disabled, sit down and discuss the situation with the employee before you take action.

- Never tolerate employees teasing their disabled peers.

CHAPTER  FIFTEEN

Things You Should Know

There are additional things you should know about employment law. They involve knowing when you need legal advice, working with attorneys, deciding when to settle a case, and testifying and being a good witness.

Avoiding Do-It-Yourself Employment Law

Seek qualified legal advice when necessary. Do not think that you can do it yourself, even if you have a good understanding of what is and is not allowed in terms of employment law.

I had a client who operated a chain of small retail stores catering to women. The performance of one store manager, Grace Marie, had dropped to below-acceptable levels. Instead of taking timely remedial action, the executive, Warren, waited until Grace Marie became pregnant and requested a leave of absence. Only then did Warren try to rid the company of the unwanted employee by installing a new store manager.

When Grace Marie was ready to return to work, Warren announced that the company had been unable to keep her position open and had found it necessary to replace her. (Warren had consulted the HR manager, who advised him that under certain circumstances he would not be required to "demote" the replacement manager upon Grace Marie's return.) Warren told Grace Marie that there were no store manager openings but offered her a job as an assistant manager until a manager's position became available. Grace Marie refused the offer and did not return to work.

This was a good defense in Warren's mind, and it might have worked at the right time in the right circumstances—had it only been true. Unfortunately, it was not true. It turned out that to avoid giving Grace Marie a manager's position, the company played "musical chairs," rotating assistant managers among stores that had no permanent manager. When this was discovered, the company's defense fell apart because it could not make a business case for its failure to reinstate Grace Marie to her former position. In my opinion, Warren—to suit his own purposes—had sought to take advantage of advice from the HR department that was an overly broad reading of the statute. The problem was compounded when Warren did not disclose the intended cover-up to either the HR department or its gullible attorney.

When you have to strain a point or parse every word of a statute or regulation to distance your acts from a particular law, it is usually an indication that you need qualified legal advice because you may be walking a very fine line and can inadvertently cross over the edge with expensive consequences. There is such a thing as being too clever, and you should not scheme to avoid the law by some type of manipulation. This is where experienced legal advice is worth the price you pay. An experienced attorney can protect you from making expensive mistakes.

Hiring an Attorney

In recent years, the legal profession has found it necessary to specialize in much the same way as the medical profession. In dealing with labor matters and employment matters (which have similarities but are not the same specialty), find a lawyer with experience because your problems should not become part of his or her learning curve. Law firms usually have a section devoted to labor and/or employment. If you seek help from such a firm, make inquiries to ensure that you will consult with a seasoned and experienced attorney.

Sometimes aggressive law firms create labor and employment sections out of whole cloth without having a core of lawyers with real expertise. Sometimes law firms hire lawyers who are less able than expected. It is thus important when you are hiring an attorney to get recommendations from other businesses and people you trust.

The more an attorney knows about you and your staff, the more cogent the advice he should be able to give. If the lawyer trusts your powers of observation, the thoroughness of your investigation, and your judgment, the more aggressive his advice should become. If you are an unknown quantity to him, the more he should question you about the facts to be relied upon. The attorney should also be familiar with business operations and have a basic understanding of how your business operates.

Avoid law firms that burden your case with too many attorneys or too few, given the relative complexity of the case. Avoid firms that change the lead attorney midstream, which generates needless expense because of duplication of effort. Competent law firms also provide you with detailed billing so you have some opportunity to appraise the reasonableness of the charges for the work performed. If you believe you are being overcharged, do not hesitate to discuss this with the attorney responsible for billing, as opposed to the subordinate attorney who may have done the work; the former may better explain the charges or reduce the bill.

Deciding Whether to Fight or Settle

The easiest advice an attorney can give is "Don't do that," urging you not to act on a particular matter. Do not settle for an attorney who gives you such advice if it goes against your own instincts, unless he can articulate clearly and persuasively exactly why you should not act. The attorney should be aggressive in helping you rid yourself of troublesome employees. When he recommends that you not discipline an employee, he should be able to give you guidance on how to proceed to reach your goal.

Some attorneys are willing to litigate to your last dollar, while others do not want the stress and strain of trying a case and will urge you to settle a claim even if it is not in your best interests. An aggressive lawyer who has your best interests in mind will not want to settle a claim that is without merit. The exception is the case where the settlement is for an insignificant amount and will be unlikely to harm the client.

Years ago, a partner taught me that trying cases was a losing proposition for a lawyer. If the case was won, he explained, the client would feel that it should have been won. If the case is lost, the client would still feel the case should have been won—and he would blame his lawyer. Nevertheless, your lawyer should be capable of giving you the benefit of his best judgment and be capable of effectively carrying out your decision if you decide to fight.

When deciding whether to fight or settle a claim, consider the following:

- The risk of losing the case
- The costs of litigation, including your attorney's fee and possibly the plaintiff's attorney's fee if the case is lost
- The loss of time by company personnel
- Whether or not settlement will encourage other employees to sue
- Whether settlement would leave a black mark against your company that could be used against you in some future but unrelated case
- Whether the passage of time during litigation might cause you to lose or transfer witnesses who are vital to the defense to distant locations
- Whether litigation or settlement could create unwanted adverse notoriety

There are no easy answers to these questions. I have experienced successful litigation that has discouraged possible litigation by others just as reasonable settlements have not created unjust claims.

One of the key elements of any successful settlement is demonstrating to other potential claimants that you are not an easy mark. To do this, you must mount a sufficiently vigorous defense so that the plaintiff's lawyer comes to realize that her case has its flaws and that settlement is preferable to wasting time trying a case she might lose (or that so little money will be made that litigation is not worthwhile). This may be accomplished easily, such as by giving a good position statement to an agency such as the EEOC, or it may be more difficult, requiring depositions and even a motion for summary judgment filed in court with all supporting documentation.

On the other hand, if the plaintiff wants only "nuisance value" for the claim, it may be best to hand over a few dollars and not waste more time on the matter. In all events, never settle without obtaining a full and complete release of both the pending claim and any other claim that might be made. Once again, it is worthwhile to engage an attorney to prepare the settlement agreement so that no other claims pop up after you settle. You may also use the agreement to obtain a confidentiality clause to keep the settlement secret as well as other things you might want to obtain from the plaintiff.

If there is more than one claim, do not settle part of the case and leave another claim outstanding; if you do so, you are only subsidizing a lawsuit against yourself. By withholding settlement, you will also create an opportunity to settle both claims for a more reasonable amount. Other factors may also warrant the refusal to settle one claim while another is pending.

Recently, a client experienced a workers compensation claim before the state industrial commission and a civil action alleging retaliation by reason of filing a workers compensation claim. The workers compensation claim was defended by an attorney hired by the insurance carrier, and I defended the civil suit. The employee and the insurance carrier's attorney wanted to settle the workers compensation claim. As part of the settlement, the claimant agreed that he was permanently disabled to the extent he could never again perform the work he was hired to do by my client. Despite this written agreement, at the civil action, he claimed that he was later cured by rest and a single treatment from a chiropractor. Fortunately, the claimant lost on the merits, but hindsight shows that it would have been better to force him to trial on the workers compensation claim so that his statement would have been under oath and perhaps subject to the written findings of a hearing officer. It would also have put pressure on the plaintiff to settle both cases at one time.

Working with an Attorney

The most valuable advice I can give you regarding working with an attorney is that you should disclose anything that possibly relates to the case. Do not withhold embarrassing or damaging facts. I never cease to be amazed by the information withheld by the client's personnel. Sometimes facts are withheld to support a person's prior judgment; sometimes they are withheld to protect someone's turf. Sooner or later, your attorney or the plaintiff's attorney will ferret out all the facts and not only could you be embarrassed but you might have done irreparable harm to the case. Sometimes clients withhold facts that support the case because in their judgment those facts are not relevant. Let your defense attorney be the judge of relevance.

Any attorney you hire should return your calls with reasonable promptness. The attorney should send you a copy of any writing he generates at the time it is submitted so that you know what he is doing and can see the quality of work being performed. The attorney should explain any reluctance to use facts you believe are relevant. Do not hesitate to question an attorney's reasoning or to make suggestions. Nobody, including the attorney, has all the answers. Every case has many nuances, and both you and your attorney should be constantly searching for answers.

One of the most difficult questions a client may ask an attorney relates to the settlement value of a particular claim. It can be hard for an attorney to recommend a settlement figure. To make the hard decisions relating to settlement, though, you need an estimate of the costs and probable outcome of litigation.

How to Be a Good Witness

There are a number of instructions I give to prospective witnesses. You should review these instructions with your own attorney to make certain she agrees with these recommendations.

The first direction is to tell the truth, but before you can do that you must know the truth. Further, if your attorney does not prepare you for specific questions you are likely to be asked, you must think of the questions you may be asked, especially on cross-examination, and think about the answers you will give. Try to think of the clearest and most powerful way you can answer those questions. Of course, the questions will probably not be posed in the way you imagine, but the exercise will enable you to formulate persuasive answers. This is also a good exercise even if you have been prepared by an attorney; if so, you should share your thoughts on the subject with her.

Be aware that in employment litigation, your attorney cannot ask "leading" questions (questions that contain an answer and generally call for a "yes" or "no" response), except with respect to preliminary questions that are without controversy. However, you may be asked leading questions on cross-examination. If so, you must be wary of two things. First, the other attorney may attempt to "put words in your mouth." Second, the other attorney may pose a series of questions that all call for the same "yes" or "no" answer, then at the end of that string may ask a question that calls for a different answer, in the hope that you inadvertently continue on with a "yes" or "no" answer out of habit and repetition.

Remember that the opposing attorney has a preconceived checklist of facts she wants to use to make her case. You must be careful not to give her the facts as she wants them but as they are in truth and in fact.

Here are the keys to effective testimony during both the deposition and trial:

- Be factually knowledgeable:

    - Review the memoranda and other documents relevant to your testimony.

    - Know the facts relevant to your testimony.

    - Be prepared to state the facts clearly and accurately.

    - Where applicable, know the underlying reasons for the facts.

- Do not use business or occupational buzzwords like "proactive."

- State the facts in detail in response to questions asked. Any conclusions that are permissible will follow the factual recitation when you are testifying on direct examination.

- Do not act ashamed of or embarrassed by the events at issue. You have done what was necessary to conduct your business; you have no apologies to make.

- Conduct yourself well on the witness stand:

    - Use good posture while on the stand. Sit up straight, do not lean back, and do not cross your legs.

    - Do not chew gum (let alone tobacco or snuff). Suppress any nervous habits.

    - Speak up in a loud, clear voice so that all can hear. Witnesses who mumble or cover their mouth with their hand are not readily understood or appreciated. In fact, if you hang your head down, talk to the floor, or cover your mouth with your hand, you can be speaking the absolute truth but everyone will think you are lying because of your body language.

- Do not eat excessively or drink alcohol during the noon recess. These things will make you drowsy and less alert.

- Respond to questions in a thoughtful, appropriate manner:

  - Listen to the question carefully; if you do not understand the question, ask that it be repeated.

  - Do not answer a question before the questioner has finished asking it. Wait at least two or three seconds between the end of the question and the start of your answer. This gives you a chance to consider your answer and also gives your attorney an opportunity to make any relevant objections. If you answer the question before he objects, he will have lost that opportunity.

  - Look directly at the questioner when answering the question.

  - Give a fair answer to the question. Do not unnaturally abbreviate your answer, but do not ramble on into irrelevant areas out of concern that something will be left unsaid. When you are being questioned by your own attorney, rely on him to bring out all the facts. If he misses anything, you can give him a note about it later and he may recall you to the stand. If you are being cross-examined and you ramble on, you open up areas of inquiry that will serve only to keep you on the stand longer and may make the case more difficult to try.

- If you do not understand a question, say so—you will not embarrass your attorney and who cares if you embarrass the plaintiff's attorney by revealing his ineptitude.

- Do not let the plaintiff's attorney "put words in your mouth" when you answer questions. This is a lawyer's phrase to cover those situations where the opposing attorney asks you a question that is part truth and part fiction, and she seeks to have you confirm both the truth and the fiction at the same time. This is where you must answer a question in your own words and say, "No, that is not the way it was" or any other appropriate preface to an answer. Be especially watchful of attorneys who try to sneak things by you. Opposing attorneys will not abuse you verbally if your lawyer is on the ball and the judge is fair minded (and they usually are on this point).

- Do not just use the words "yes" or "no" unless those words are the perfect answer to the question. If you abbreviate your answers by using just "yes" or "no," you may be accepting matters that are not factual or negating matters that are factual. Especially on cross-examination, you may find it necessary to tell the attorney or the judge something along the lines of, "I can't answer your question the way it is phrased" or "Your question is partially true and partially untrue." Once you make this kind of statement, it is clear to the court and jury that you are not being evasive but only trying to be precise.

- This is not a test of your memory. If you have notes, business documents, and other material with you, don't hesitate to use them when answering questions. If you don't know an answer but believe it is contained in such documents and the documents are in the courtroom, ask to see them. Your attorney will supply these things to you, and if the plaintiff's attorney refuses such a request, she stands revealed as someone who is up to a rascally trick and any inability to answer will not harm your case because your attorney can put the documents before you on redirect examination.

- If you are asked a question and you don't know the answer, your attorney may then ask something like "Are there any documents that would refresh your memory?" That is your opportunity to say "Yes, if I could see the Disciplinary Report (or whatever else), I think I could answer your question." That enables your counsel to present that document to you and for you to read the document. He would then ask if you have refreshed your memory. If your memory is refreshed, you simply say "yes," and then he will ask you to answer the question.

- When on the stand, do not speculate. The law does not require you to engage in guesswork. The court expects you to testify truthfully about facts within your knowledge. By not guessing at answers you do not know, you do not put your company at risk. Some areas of unwise speculation are:

    - What your company would do in a given circumstance.

    - What someone else would do in a given circumstance.

    - What someone else knows about a specific fact (as opposed to broad knowledge of the event or a given subject such as job duties, manufacturing processes, etc.).

- On whether or not there exists records proving or disproving anything.

- On what you would do under a hypothetical circumstance.

- By not guessing at answers you do not know, you do not put your company at risk. This is particularly true of documents. You may think a record exists of a certain thing, but unless you are positive as to the existence of that record and you can go lay your hands on that record upon request, don't be eager to agree that there is such a record. Otherwise, your attorney will have to go to all the trouble of proving that you were wrong, and that detracts from your credibility.

- Similarly, you shouldn't give an opinion on what you might do in hypothetical circumstances unless it is within your area of knowledge or expertise and you know full well exactly what you would do in that particular event. Quite often, in a circumstance that is unfamiliar, you would find it necessary to discuss the matter with your supervisor or with the Human Resources Department or Legal Department; the matter might well be the subject of a committee meeting, or any number of things. Therefore, don't be hasty and jump to conclusions that are not real facts but poorly conceived opinions about an event that has yet to occur.

- Listen to objections, especially those made by your attorney. While objections are perfectly legal and proper, they may also suggest things that are factually wrong with the question being asked of you on cross-examination. Do not rush to answer a question when an objection is pending. Wait for the court to rule because it may well be in your favor.

- Be aware that if an objection is sustained, you don't have to answer the question. If the objection is overruled, you must answer the question to the best of your ability, but having heard the objection, you can be on guard.

- Here are some examples of objections that might be made and that you should listen for:

  - *"Counsel is misstating the facts."* This means that you should be alert for opposing counsel trying to put words in your mouth.

  - *"Counsel is misstating the witness's prior testimony."* This means that you should be alert for opposing counsel trying to develop a contradiction where none exists. The prior testimony of previous witnesses may also be misquoted to you on cross-examination and this will be subject to the same objection.

  - *"The question calls for speculation."*

  - *"The question calls for a conclusion."*

  - *"There's no proper foundation for the question"* or *"The question assumes facts not in evidence."* This often indicates that counsel is assuming certain facts not in evidence (because they are not facts or otherwise inadmissible). Opposing counsel may use this tactic to get into evidence things that would otherwise be inadmissible on grounds of relevance or because he has no evidence from his own witnesses to prove those facts.

- *"The question is argumentative."* You should not be expected to argue the case, but if you are asked and compelled to answer a question such as "When did you stop beating your wife?" you have to say, "I cannot answer the question the way it is phrased."

- *"The question was previously asked and answered."* This is a signal to you that the opposing attorney is repeating the question and hoping that you will be foolish enough to offer a different answer. (Of course, if you made a mistake in your previous answer, this would be a good opportunity to correct it and explain that you misunderstood the previous question or whatever circumstances apply.)

- *"The question is unintelligible."* If your attorney does not understand the question, make sure you do.

- *"This is a double question."* This refers to a question calling for you to answer two different questions posed at one time. If a double question gets by your attorney, make certain you indicate which part of the question you are answering with each part of your reply.

- Again, if the objection is sustained, you don't have to answer the question. If the objection is overruled, you must answer the question to the best of your ability, but having heard the objection, you can be on guard.

- Be on the alert for trick questions. There are no trick questions if you know the facts, except for the following:

  - *"Did you discuss your testimony with anyone?"* The answer is, of course, "Yes. I discussed it with the company attorney." There is nothing wrong with this. It is legally permissible and usually expected.

- *"Did your attorney tell you what to say?"* Of course he should not tell you what to say. He should tell you only to know the facts and tell the truth. That having been said, there are numerous ways to recite the same set of facts. There is nothing wrong with your attorney helping you state true facts in the most effective way possible.

- *"Are you being paid to testify here today?"* The best answer I ever heard was a witness who said, "I certainly hope so." You are on salary if you are a company employee, and if you are an hourly worker, you are entitled to be reimbursed for lost time. If you are not a company employee, the company attorney should be willing to reimburse you or your employer for any lost time or expenses. This is a legally permissible act.

- During recesses, before and after the trial day begins, do not laugh, joke, or be friendly with the plaintiff or his attorney, especially in front of the jury. It is okay to be civil, but do all you can to avoid exchanging words with the other side so that you cannot be quoted or misquoted.

Scheduling issues should be worked out with your attorney. There is seldom need to shut down your business operations in order to have all witnesses present.

All of this seems like much to remember; however, being prepared for trial will lessen the stress of being in the courtroom and will lend credibility to the defense. You should share this advice with all other prospective witnesses on your side of the case so that they too may be prepared.

Employer's Legal Pad—Chapter Fifteen Checklist

- When hiring an attorney, look for one with a lot of experience in labor and/or employment law. Don't be on the wrong end of someone else's learning curve.

- Disclose everything to your attorney that might possibly be relevant to the case.

- Before you testify, review all written records thoroughly to refresh your memory.

- Before you testify in court or give a deposition, take some time to review the witness stand instructions presented in this chapter with your attorney.

- Before settlement or any settlement conference, assess the strengths and weakness of your case, the pros and cons of settlement, and the ramifications of trial.

Final Thoughts

I recently read an article quoting a plaintiff's lawyer who said that 80 percent of all employment claims filed in federal court were dismissed as being without merit. This certainly harmonizes with my experience and that of my firm. While this is good news, if true, the fact remains that time and expense was involved in ridding the courts of all those cases without merit. The bad news is that the plaintiff's bar is now turning to the state courts for damages. State court judges, including appellate judges, do not have the advantage of the thirty years of litigation experienced by the federal courts, nor do state court judges have one or more graduate lawyers working as law clerks to help them research and write opinions. State courts are usually not receptive to motions for summary judgment, whereas such motions are expected, if not welcome, in federal courts. Finally, state court judges may be elected and may be beholden to the plaintiffs' bar in their jurisdiction who fund their reelection campaigns. They may also be dependent for their election on voters who have negative feelings toward business, all of which adversely impact the business community defending employment discrimination claims. For these reasons, the need to be prepared continues for the foreseeable future.

Preventive measures can help you avoid the gut-wrenching discomfort of litigation, but if your best effort fails, the importance of having preserved evidence you can rely upon is obvious. Few things are worse than sitting in court watching the facts you relied upon leak away or be diminished in value by cross-examination or convincing evidence presented by the opposition. The importance of rational, measured decision making supported by the facts relied upon is also critical. This is not to say that you should not make a necessary decision simply because there is a credibility dispute, but it is to say that if your facts are fairly bulletproof, they will support your decision and prevent embarrassment upon trial. Remember also the need to project the fact that you acted fairly and reasonably in the given circumstance, which could only have been done if you were in fact fair, consistent, and reasonable.

If you do these things, you will have gone far in preventing an adverse court judgment. Even if you lose, you will no doubt have helped keep the damages at an amount less than might have been assessed by a court or jury. Going into the fight prepared gives you great advantage from the very beginning and helps you keep that advantage right through to the end.

Summary of Key Employment Laws

This description of key employment laws is not meant to provide a comprehensive review of all the terms and nuances of those laws. This summary is not expansive, nor does it contain all aspects of each law. The purpose of this book is to prepare you to deal with employment problems and make you aware of potential problems rather than to enable you to interpret the laws on your own. Bear in mind that employment discrimination is not limited to hiring, firing, promotion, demotion, pay practices, and transfers. Discrimination entails any practice that materially has an adverse effect upon an employee or job applicant.

As the example of Grace Marie, the pregnant store manager in Chapter 15, demonstrates, it is very difficult to avoid legal proscriptions by creative thinking, and such acts are seldom successful when all the facts are examined during the legal process. Also remember that there are usually state laws covering the same types of discrimination forbidden by federal law, and the state laws are sometimes more far-reaching than the comparable federal statutes. An example is discrimination based upon sexual orientation, which is not unlawful under federal law but may be under your state's law. You should therefore make certain you are familiar with state statutes governing the employment relationship. Finally, remember that the law does not require preference for any of these factors (with the possible exception of government contractors with affirmative action plans that may require the employer to more actively seek out persons in a protected classification for certain jobs), only that there be no discrimination.

Age Discrimination in Employment Act (ADEA). 29 United States Code §621 et seq. An act protecting the employment rights of persons over forty years of age. See also the *Older Workers Benefit Protection Act* (Pul.L.101-433 § 1) if you intend to reach any settlement agreement of an employment claim involving a worker over age forty. The greatest problems are posed by long-service employees who are replaced by younger workers. A fifty-five-year-old replaced by a fifty-three-year-old may theoretically have a claim, but it will be unlikely to have legal merit.

Americans with Disabilities Act (ADA). 42 United States Code §12101 et seq. An act protecting the rights, including employment rights, of qualified individuals with physical and mental impairments, a record of such impairments, or regarded as being impaired. Such persons must be able to perform the essential functions of the employment position held or desired, with or without reasonable accommodation. The ADA is so vague that it is not always evident whether or not impairment exists that comes within the protection of the statute. Compliance with this law requires nondiscrimination in the form of reasonable accommodation, among other things.

Civil Rights Act of 1964 as amended, sometimes referred to as *Title VII* or the *Equal Employment Act.* 42 United States Code §2000e et seq. An act that makes unlawful employment discrimination based upon race, sex, color, religion, and national origin. Age and disability discrimination laws incorporate by reference portions of this statute. Charges must be filed within 180 or 300 days of the discriminatory event, depending upon whether or not there is a state civil rights act. The act applies to employers who employ fifteen or more employees for each working day in each of twenty or more weeks in the current or preceding calendar year.

Civil Rights Act of 1866 as amended in 1991. 42 United States Code §1981 et seq. An act that originally prohibited discrimination in the making of contracts. It was amended in 1991 to include performance, modification, and termination of contracts and to provide for compensatory and punitive damages in amounts ranging from $50,000 to $300,000, depending upon the number of people employed. The act also provides a basis for jury trials.

Equal Pay Act. 29 United States Code §206 (d). An act that requires that employees be paid equally without regard to sex for work that requires equal skill, effort, and responsibility performed under similar conditions. Exceptions are made when pay is made pursuant to a seniority system, a merit system, a system that measures earnings by quantity and quality, or a differential other than sex.

Family and Medical Leave Act (FMLA). 29 United States Code §2601 et seq. An act that provides for an unpaid medical leave of absence of up to twelve weeks for employees who have been employed twelve months and have 1,250 hours of service within the previous twelve months. The FMLA applies to employers having fifty or more employees within seventy-five miles of the worksite and working each day of twenty calendar workweeks in the current or preceding year. The regulations interpreting this act are voluminous and should be consulted if there is any real question concerning medical necessity.

Mine Safety and Health Act (MSHA) 30 U.S.C. §801. An act that applies to mines. See *Occupational Safety and Health Act.*

Occupational Safety and Health Act (OSHA). 29 United States Code §651 et seq. A statute that sets forth specific health and safety regulations for industry and business. It is relevant here because employees who file complaints with or against their company regarding compliance have job protection from employer retaliation.

Older Workers Benefit Protection Act (OWBPA). A section of the *Age Discrimination in Employment Act* (29 United States Code §626). It sets forth specific conditions that must be met before an actual or potential settlement of an age discrimination claim will be binding upon an older worker. A failure to comply means that the employee has your money and you have not resolved the claim.

Pregnancy Discrimination Act (PDA). 42 United States Code §2000e(k). An amendment to the Civil Rights Act of 1964 that prohibits intentional discrimination against pregnant employees and the maintenance of a policy that adversely affects pregnant employees.

Uniformed Services Employment and Reemployment Rights Act (USERRA). 43 United States Code §4301 et seq. An act that provides employment protection for persons serving in the armed forces, their reserve components, and the National Guard. Enlistment and calls to active duty are protected for up to five years and in some cases even longer. Employees are required to apply for reinstatement within ninety days of discharge. There are stringent rules relating to the veteran's restoration to a particular position in the workforce.

Glossary of Terms

These definitions and descriptions are mostly those of the author and are meant to harmonize with the message of this book. In some instances, the definitions could be made broader or more specific, but I believe that they will be of more value to the reader as stated.

actual damages   The amount of actual monetary damage suffered by a party.

adverse action   Any action taken by an employer where an employee suffers an adverse (detrimental) effect. Adverse actions include discharges, layoffs, demotions, suspensions, docking, and other acts of discipline.

adverse impact   A doctrine that implies unlawful discrimination because a particular rule or practice disproportionately affects persons in a protected class and cannot be justified by a reasonable, nondiscriminatory factor.

attorney fees   Fees that courts are permitted to award to the attorney of the prevailing party, in accord with most antidiscrimination employment laws. These fees are based upon the area standards for attorney's hourly rates times hours expended plus costs and other relevant expenses.

at-will employment   An employment agreement whereby either party may terminate the employment relationship at any time.

back pay   Pay for the period of time starting with the loss of pay until the employee is reinstated or the case is settled.

bona fide occupational qualification (BFOQ)   A factor that an employer may rely on to show that a particular religion, sex, or national origin is reasonably necessary to achieve normal operations.

charge   A formal document filed with a state or federal agency tasked to address acts alleged to be discriminatory.

circumstantial evidence   Evidence allowed in court that permits an inference to be made.

Civil Rights Act(s)   Federal and/or state legislation that protects certain civil rights, including employment rights, with respect to race, color, sex, religion, and national origin. Some states have broadened these rights to include other things such as sexual orientation.

compensatory damages   In employment law cases, damages that are to compensate for future monetary losses and nonmonetary losses, including emotional pain, suffering, inconvenience, mental anguish, and loss of enjoyment of life.

constructive discharge   A circumstance that usually occurs when an employee quits claiming intolerable working conditions. Constructive discharge is implied when working conditions are such that no reasonable person could be expected to continue in employment.

defendant   The corporation, person, or legal entity being sued.

deposition   The taking of testimony under oath before a court reporter who reduces the testimony to writing (the deposition may be videotaped as an alternative or in addition to traditional reporting). Unless a party or friendly witness is deposed by the party's own attorney, the deposition is taken in the form of cross-examination. No judge is present to rule upon relevance or other issues; thus, preparation is essential so that the person being deposed will not give a deposition at variance with his trial testimony.

direct evidence   Evidence that permits a party plaintiff to claim that it proves intent (or action) was unlawful without having to show that the employee was the victim of disparate treatment or disparate impact. In the context of employment discrimination, this usually means that the employer or its agents either admitted that it relied upon a prohibited factor such as race or sex or used or tolerated abusive language that implies that bigotry or intolerance were present.

discovery   A legal process in civil actions whereby each side seeks to discover what the other party intends to prove during trial. This usually involves depositions, interrogatories, and requests to produce documents or other physical evidence.

discrimination   In simplest terms, this is to treat one person differently from another person who is in a comparable situation (sometimes the term "similarly situated" is used). Discrimination becomes unlawful when the reason for differentiation is based upon unlawful reasons such as race, sex, age, etc.

disparate treatment   When the plaintiff complains that his treatment by the employer was different from that of "similarly situated" employees because of his age, race, sex, disability, etc.

EEOC   The U.S. Equal Employment Opportunity Commission, the agency empowered to investigate and prosecute claims of employment discrimination involving race, color, sex, religion, national origin, age, and disability. Regardless of the merits of any particular claim, the EEOC issues a right-to-sue letter, which entitles the employee to file a civil action within ninety days of issuance. State agencies with a similar charter may be established in your state by reason of state law.

emotional distress   A claim for monetary damages to compensate the employee for anxiety and other emotions experienced as a result of the defendant's actions.

employment discrimination   Acting in a manner that distinguishes between employees and applicants for reasons that are made unlawful by statute or regulation. This concerns wages, hours, and conditions of employment such as hiring, firing, promotion, and transfer.

examination   At trial witnesses are subject to direct examination, cross examination by the opposing party, and redirect examination by their own attorney. Redirect examination is often confined to matters raised in cross examination.

false charges   Charges made that are totally untrue and may even constitute perjury. If you believe someone has made false charges against you, you are in need of legal representation before you act because a strict and high standard of proof is required of any employer who relies upon this claim to take disciplinary action.

front pay   Damages sought in lieu of reinstatement, usually pay and benefits for a period of time or until presumed retirement.

hearsay   An out-of-court statement by someone other than the person testifying that is not an admission against interest (this being an exception to the rule excluding hearsay).

indirect evidence   Evidence that is relevant enough to allow a judge or jury to infer unlawful motivation in an employment discrimination case.

interrogatories Written questions posed by one party involved in a lawsuit to the opposing party that must be answered under oath. These questions may be detailed and require considerable research to answer correctly. Answers may be used against a party if the question is relevant to the issue being tried.

negative reference The making of unfavorable remarks concerning a present or former employee to a prospective employer. Note that the courts have not considered truth as a defense to a charge of retaliation based upon a negative reference, and some courts have allowed a plaintiff to claim that a performance evaluation was unfairly prepared and thereby impeded future employment opportunities.

NLRB The National Labor Relations Board, the agency that enforces the National Labor Relations Act. That act provides the procedure for certifying and decertifying labor unions as the exclusive bargaining representatives of a group of employees. It also prohibits certain conduct by management and labor that are deemed unfair labor practices such as discharge for union or protected activities, secondary boycotts, and refusals to bargain in good faith, among other things.

plaintiff The person bringing a civil action.

preemptory strike Blocking certain individuals from being seated as part of a jury. In a jury trial, prospective jurors are brought before the court and interviewed by the court and/or the attorneys representing the parties. Each party to a civil action is permitted to strike a designated number of jurors from the initial panel selected for any reason other than sex or race. After preemptory strikes are exhausted, a party must show a good reason for asking the court to remove any other prospective juror.

pretext   In employment discrimination cases, a reason given for the employer's action to mask or obscure the true reason for acting.

prevailing party   In the context of employment discrimination, means the side that wins. For a plaintiff to be the prevailing party, he needs to win only a single allegation regardless of how many separate claims are made. While Title VII of the Civil Rights Act plainly provides for the awarding of attorney fees to the prevailing party, the U.S. Supreme Court read the rights of defendants out of that statute unless the plaintiff's suit was "frivolous, unreasonable, or without foundation." See *Christiansburg Garment Co. v. EEOC*, 434 U.S. 412, at 421 (1978). See also *Texas State Teachers Assn. v. Garland Independent School District*, 489 U.S. 782 (1989).

prima facie **case**   When there is a sufficient legal claim to require the defendant to present its defense. Note that the presentation of a valid defense does not mean that the case will be dismissed. In employment discrimination cases, the former employee will have an opportunity to attack the defense as pretext or not the true reason and to otherwise show that there was a discriminatory motive involved.

protected activity   Activity on the part of an employee that is entitled to legal protection against discrimination in the workplace.

protected concerted activity   A concept of the National Labor Relations Act that affords protection to two or more people acting in concert with respect to issues concerning wages, hours, and working conditions.

punitive damages   An amount sought by a plaintiff on the theory that the defendant's actions were so outrageous and unreasonable that a sum of money should be awarded in a sufficient amount to discourage further misconduct. The federal standard in employment law cases is whether the defendant acted "with malice or reckless indifference to . . . federally protected rights. . . ." State laws probably have a similar but not necessarily identical test. Note that a plaintiff's attorney will seek to determine the company's net worth so that it may be placed in evidence and used to assess the amount of the punitive damage award; this demand will generate substantial legal controversy in most instances.

request to produce   A form of legal discovery allowed in most cases where one party calls upon the opposing party to produce specific physical items. In the context of employment discrimination cases, this usually means personnel and financial records.

retaliation   An action taken against an employee to get even for the employee's having made a claim of employment discrimination concerning himself or others.

summary judgment   A measure a defense attorney (and on occasion plaintiff's attorney) can take to seek final judgment in a case before trial, showing that there is no material dispute of facts and under the circumstances the moving party is entitled to a favorable judgment as a matter of law.

tort   A civil wrong for which an action may be brought.

vicarious liability   A phrase used in holding employers liable for the acts of its managers and supervisors, usually in the context of sexual harassment cases, even if higher level of management had no active involvement in or knowledge of the incident. The laws against employment discrimination impose strict liability for the acts of supervisors and managers who are in a direct line of authority over the employee. However, since it is difficult to distance the supervisor or manager from the employee when in litigation, a far better practice is to ensure that all persons in authority behave in an appropriate manner.

whistle-blowing   The act of an employee reporting his employer for a violation of a state or federal law. As with all claims of employer retaliation, the report need not be correct. This also includes protests within the company itself and need not be confined to state or federal employees.

Quick Reference Guide

If you are faced with an emergency situation and do not wish to thumb through this book to figure out what to do, here is an outline of immediate actions you should take.

- Interview all participants and witnesses to the incident and learn the *who, what, when, where,* and *why* of the situation.

- Have all participants and witnesses put their statements in writing. Have them sign off on their written statements.

- If the witnesses will not write out their statements themselves, you should do it instead and then ask them to review the statement for accuracy. After the witness agrees and any necessary corrections have been made ask them to sign off on each page to signify agreement with its accuracy.

- Confront the offending employee with the accusations (if you have not already taken this step) and learn her defenses or excuses. Ideally, the employee should put her defenses and excuses in written form.

- Review all relevant facts as related, all relevant rules, and any physical evidence.

- Engage in clear-cut, incisive thinking about what you believe to be appropriate action.

- Review recent disciplinary history to determine if your contemplated action is inconsistent with prior discipline and company rules and policies and/or is discriminatory for some unlawful reason.

- Note and preserve evidence of any prior consistent action on the part of the company.

- Make certain that the action you intend to take is not inconsistent with previous evaluations of the employee.

- Make certain that the action you intend to take is not inconsistent with any contract or agreement you have made with the employee.

- Check to see if the employee's actions are protected concerted or union activity or if the employee was protesting unlawful discrimination, harassment, or safety problems. Any of these things warrant a call to your attorney. The reason for recommending the opinion of an attorney is that each of these things may have legal protection against discrimination and make discipline unlawful. This does not necessarily mean that you cannot take action but it may have a bearing on the manner in which you deal with the problem.

- Consider how a perfect stranger might judge your decision and your reasons for making that decision. If your decision might appear unduly harsh or inherently unfair, rethink it to make certain your reasoning is solid.

- Confront the employee and tell him your decision and precisely why you reached it. (This does not require you to disclose each and every fact, only the ultimate facts that led to your decision.)

- Try to have a witness at the meeting with the employee. Both you and the witness should make good notes about what is said, by whom, and in what order.

- Avoid off-the-cuff discussions or telephone conversations with the employee. Be prepared for any confrontation with her that might occur.

- Preserve all evidence, at least until any relevant statutes of limitations have expired and longer if possible because the doctrine of "continuing violations" may allow a plaintiff to reach back for many years. Some of the more common limitations periods are:

- *National Labor Relations Board.* Six months.

- *Equal Employment Opportunity Commission.* Three hundred days, but continuing violations may have a life span of several years.

- *State civil rights statutes.* Usually six months or 180 days.

- *U.S. Department of Labor wage/hour issues.* Two years except for willful violations, which have a three-year limitation.

- *Statutory actions such as workers compensation retaliation.* Usually two to three years, but each state has a different period of limitation so if there is an issue, check the law.

- *Tort actions.* Vary from state to state.

Sample Consent Form for Electronic Monitoring

It is a good idea to get the consent of your employees for electronic monitoring, using a form such as the one presented here. Note that this form has not been tested in litigation, although it is believed to be complete in all respects. Have your attorney review the form to ensure that it protects all company activities subject to monitoring and surveillance. Your attorney should also check for any applicable amendments to the law or court decisions made after the publication of this book.

* * *

In consideration for my employment or continued employment, I understand and agree to abide by the published policy of this company regarding electronic communications by telephone, voice-mail, facsimile, e-mail, or any other means or device. I also understand and agree that the company policy may be amended from time to time and I agree to abide by the amended policy as well.

I specifically agree that e-mail transmissions to and from me as well as all electronically stored materials are subject to monitoring. I recognize that company computers may not be used for improper purposes including but not limited to the following:

- Personal uses such as games and personal communications

- Acts of sabotage against any person or institution

- In breach of matters confidential to this company or any other company including trade secrets, manufacturing processes, and customer lists

- Any act of disloyalty to this company

- Disparagement of this company, its customers, or employees of either

- To harass or discriminate against any person, which includes acts of mockery

- To insult or defame any person or company

- To infringe upon any copyright or patent

- Any unlawful act

I recognize that my telephone, facsimile, e-mail, and voice-mail communications may be monitored to ensure that I am complying with company policies. I recognize that such monitoring may include personal communications and consequently I do not expect privacy in such matters absent specific written agreement by management to defer to my privacy.

Surveillance by means of videotape and related equipment, Global Positioning Systems, and cell phone tracking is in place or may be instituted at some future time and I agree to accept the foregoing as part of the consideration for my employment or continued employment.

Employee Signature: _____

Date: _____

Sample Rules of Conduct

It is a good idea to have rules of conduct (such as those presented here) that are distributed to all employees to alert them about what behavior is and is not allowed in your company. Remember that all policies applicable to a union-organized facility require negotiation with the union before implementation unless a collective bargaining agreement gives the company the specific right to determine such policy. The obligation to negotiate in good faith does not require that the company and union reach agreement; however, the union contract may make such requirement. You should contact a competent labor attorney if there is any issue about your rights and obligations in this regard.

*   *   *

The following rules of conduct are designed for the safe and harmonious operation of the company. While these rules may seem voluminous, they are not all-inclusive. There are other specific policies concerning _____ [list any applicable policies, such as those regarding attendance, sexual and other forms of harassment, drug and alcohol abuse, and electronic communications, that you may have

185

published separately] that must also be followed. Violations of these rules will result in discipline up to and including discharge.

It is important to exercise courtesy and good judgment at all times. If you conduct yourself as a conscientious employee, it is unlikely that you will experience a serious disciplinary problem. Discipline will depend upon the nature of the misconduct, any resultant harm, prior work and disciplinary record, length of service, and any mitigating factors that may be present.

The following are forbidden:

- Physical or verbal abuse of employees, customers, or service providers at any time. This rule includes the making of threats as well as attempts to intimidate and fighting.

- Falsification of any company record including but not limited to employment applications, time cards, or reports.

- Insubordination, which includes the intentional refusal to follow instructions as well as intemperate remarks.

- Use of obscene, profane, or abusive language while on company time or on company premises.

- Gambling on company premises.

- Smoking in any unauthorized area.

- Loafing, sleeping on the job, or any willful idleness when work is to be performed.

- Theft, fraud, or any act of dishonesty concerning the company, its employees, its customers, or its service providers at any time.

- Failure to comply with the company dress code or to maintain a satisfactory level of personal hygiene.

- Commission of a felony on or off company premises.

- Violation of any safety rule.

- Violation of the rule against harassment and sexual harassment.

- Violation of the attendance policy.

- Violation of the drug and alcohol abuse policy.

- Violation of the electronic communications policy.

- Violation of any rule regarding the solicitation or distribution of literature.

- Leaving the assigned work area without permission.

- Interfering with the work of other employees.

- Immoral, indecent, or disorderly conduct while on company premises.

- Discourteous conduct toward management or customers or members of the public with whom you are interacting as an employee of the company.

- Possession of weapons including firearms, knives, and clubs, concealed or otherwise, while on company property. (You may wish to exclude such things if they are locked in a vehicle, including unloaded firearms.)

- Possession of alcohol or illegal substances on company property.

- Failure to advise management of any legal substance taken that may affect the ability to work properly and safely.

- Horseplay or the creation of an unsafe or unsanitary condition while on company property.

- Unauthorized possession of property belonging to the company, a visitor, or another employee.

- Negligent or deliberate destruction of property belonging to the company, a visitor, or another employee.

- Violation of any policy regarding confidentiality of company records, customers, or methods of production.

- Incompetence or the failure to work at the expected level of performance.

- Any act considered detrimental to the company, its employees or customers, or members of the public.

Sample Drug and Alcohol Testing Policy

The following is a sample drug and alcohol testing policy that you can implement in your workplace.

Objective

It is the objective of _____ [insert company name] to establish and maintain a workplace that is free from the use and effects of illegal drugs and alcohol.

Policy

[Company name] prohibits the possession, use, sale, or distribution of illegal drugs or alcohol during working hours or while on company premises, including parking lots, or reporting to work or being on the job under the influence of illegal drugs or alcohol. An employee with a positive test result shall be deemed to be under the influence.

Employees found using or possessing drugs or alcohol on company premises are subject to immediate discharge without the necessity of testing or lesser discipline.

Preemployment Testing

Applicants for employment will be required to undergo urinalysis or other screening for illegal drugs. The applicant shall be informed of and consent to this drug screening prior to the screening. Refusal by an applicant to submit to a test shall result in denial of employment. When the presence of an illegal drug is detected in the job applicant, employment will be denied or revoked.

Testing of Employees

The company shall have the right to require that an employee submit to urinalysis and/or other screening methods for illegal drugs and alcohol under the following circumstances:

1. On a random basis for illegal drugs only, once per year. (Selection will be done randomly by an outside medical services provider.)

2. Following any injury in the workplace in which an employee is involved and which requires medical treatment and/or evaluation by a physician.

3. Where the company has reasonable suspicion that the employee is under the influence of and/or has recently ingested illegal drugs and/or alcohol.

In addition to alcohol and drug testing, the company may take a number of other steps to ensure that this policy is followed. These steps may include periodic searches of company property and premises, including but not limited to lunch boxes, toolboxes, vehicles, desks, and work areas. Refusal to cooperate with these procedures shall subject an employee to immediate discharge.

Laboratory

The company shall designate the physician, healthcare institution, clinic, and/or laboratory to be utilized as well as any changes in persons or institutions involved in the testing process. The company shall be responsible for the expense incurred in testing.

Testing Procedures

Each employee to be tested pursuant to this policy shall:

- Cooperate fully.
- Execute and complete truthfully such documents and releases as may be required by the physician, healthcare institution, clinic, and/or laboratory.
- Authorize a written report of the results and/or other relevant records to be submitted to the company.

All initially positive drug screens will be confirmed.

The following are grounds for immediate discharge:

1. Failure or refusal to cooperate in all phases of the testing procedure

2. Failure or refusal to promptly submit to such examinations and/or tests

3. Failure or refusal to execute proper consent forms

4. Suspected adulteration or tampering with a specimen

Examples of suspected adulteration or tampering include but are not limited to a specimen temperature outside the acceptable range, presence of foreign objects or material in the specimen, or a specimen that is reported as dilute.

Positive Test Result

An employee who has been tested for alcohol or illegal drugs and whose test proves positive will be discharged or referred to rehabilitation at the discretion of the company.* If rehabilitation is offered or required, it will be offered or required in conjunction with the first violation of this policy, and the employee must successfully complete the rehabilitation program in order to return to work.

An employee who returns to work following a rehabilitation program will be subject to random testing for a period of thirty-six (36) months after returning to work.

Under no circumstances will any employee be offered more than one opportunity at rehabilitation. A second positive test result will result in immediate termination.

Voluntary Rehabilitation

An employee may request a medical leave of absence for the purpose of undergoing treatment pursuant to an approved program for alco-

---

*Whether to discharge for the first offense and make no provision for rehabilitation is a policy decision the employer must make. It is recommended that you fire any probationary employee

holism or drug abuse. This leave of absence must be requested prior to a positive test result or the commission of any act subject to disciplinary action.

Such leave of absence shall be granted on a onetime basis and shall be for a maximum of thirty (30) days unless extended by mutual agreement.

This voluntary rehabilitation shall not apply to probationary employees.

Conviction of a Drug-Related Offense

Any employee convicted in any manner and regardless of sentence of a drug-related offense shall be subject to discipline, including discharge, without testing and without the opportunity of rehabilitation. This rule includes but is not limited to:

- The manufacture of illegal substances
- The sale of illegal substances
- The possession of illegal substances outside the workplace
- Possession of drug-related paraphernalia

Acknowledgment of Receipt of Substance Abuse Policy

I, the undersigned, hereby acknowledge I have received a copy of the _____ [insert company name] Substance Abuse Policy.

Employee Signature: _____

Date: _____

---

who tests positive on the first offense, just as you might wish to fire any employee caught using alcohol or drugs during working time.

Sample No-Fault Attendance Policy

"No fault" is something of a misnomer for an attendance policy but the term is meant to convey the idea that a prohibited number of absences and tardies will result in discipline even if the employee claims to be without fault for some or all of the occurrences. When you title the policy simply refer to it as the "Company Attendance Policy." Use a form such as the one below to inform your employees of your company's attendance policy.

* * *

Scheduling the workload and staffing the workplace are very important functions that have a great effect on both the budget and completion of work on schedule. Unanticipated absences have an adverse impact on our company, so we are asking you to assist us by helping us minimize the problems created by absenteeism. We recognize that almost every employee gives the greatest possible cooperation by coming to work on time and avoiding all but the most unavoidable absences, but unfortunately, from time to time a problem develops that requires an effective remedy. In an effort to treat all employees fairly and to avoid penalizing the conscientious employee who has a temporary problem, we have developed a "no-fault" attendance policy that we believe will accomplish those ends. "No fault" means that excuses are unacceptable, except as allowed by law or specifically identified in this policy. As always, if you have or anticipate attendance problems, by all means contact your supervisor to see what arrangements, if any, can be made to accommodate your problem.

Definitions

For purposes of this policy, an "absence" is defined as absence from work for half or more of a scheduled workday. A "tardy" or "leave early" is an absence of less than half of the scheduled workday, at the beginning or end of the workday. [Here, you should insert any grace period you wish to allow at the beginning or end of the workday.]

Basic Obligations

You are expected to notify _____ [insert name of person] of any absence or tardiness as soon as possible. Reports are to be made each day an absence or tardiness occurs. Unreported absences or tardy events will be treated as an "absence without leave" (AWOL) and considered a serious violation of policy. If it becomes necessary to leave early, you should notify your supervisor as soon as the need becomes known. Notice should be made by the employee. Notice from other persons will not be accepted if the employee was physically able to make the notification.

Employees absent for three (3) days without report shall be automatically terminated. If a failure to report is due to circumstances beyond the control of the employee, the employee may be reinstated without penalty. [Here you may want to add that incarceration is not an acceptable excuse.] Remember your obligation is to report personally as soon as possible.

How the Policy Works

Counseling and disciplinary action will be taken whenever an employee's absences and/or tardy and leave early events exceed the allowable point level in the designated time frame. AWOLs will be assessed 2 points, absences with report will be assessed 1 point, and tardiness and leaving early will each be assessed $1/2$ point.

The table below indicates the appropriate action to be taken when an employee reaches the level shown within any consecutive twelve-month period.* (Note that you must insert in the table the point levels you determine to be appropriate.)

Point level	*Action*
X	First written warning
XX	Second written warning
XXX	Disciplinary layoff of _____ days without pay
XXXX	Discharge

Employees who have been disciplined but subsequently work _____ [insert number of months here, e.g., 6, 12] months without further

---

*You must determine the acceptable level of absenteeism in your company. If you find that your system is too rigid, you may rewrite and republish the policy and perhaps clear employees' records of the last discipline taken. If you find that your system is too lax, you may rewrite and republish the new standards while taking steps to ensure that a disciplinary step is not unfairly accelerated by subtracting a point or points or installing a grace period where the old policy remains in effect. In either case, make certain that all employees know of the change in policy.

discipline will have their record cleared. Employees who have been disciplined but subsequently work _____ [insert number of months here; this should be half the level necessary for complete clearing of the record] months without further discipline but who exceed the allowable point level will repeat the previous disciplinary step.

Excused Absences

Excused absences will not be assessed points. Merely reporting an absence does not mean that it will be excused, however fewer points are assessed than in cases of unreported (AWOL) absences. Excused absences are limited to the following:

- FMLA-approved leave (it is the employee's obligation to apply for FMLA leave, so be certain to apply to avoid the assessment of points)

- Vacations, holidays, and other approved leaves

- Layoff resulting from lack of work

- Disciplinary layoffs

- Absences related to on-the-job injury

- Authorized leaves of absence

- Required court appearances such as jury duty or being summoned as a witness (note that personal appearances for criminal matters will not be excused; personal appearances for the employee's own civil matters require the requesting and receipt of approved leave)

- Severe weather as determined by the company

- Two absences per calendar year when absence is supported by a physician's note certifying the date of treatment provided also: (1) the absence is for three (3) scheduled days of work or less, and (2) there is a genuine medical reason for the absence (note that when medical appointments are made in advance, the absence must be reported in advance). (This part of the policy may be a good idea where there is a problem with employees being frequently absent and presenting a health provider's note as an excuse. If the company provides a given number of sick days it may not want to accept a doctor's note for casual absences and should make it clear to employees that once sick days are used up they will be assessed points unless the absence qualifies as an excused absence.)

- Any excuse mandated by state law.

Clearing the Record of Points

If no points are assessed within a calendar month, $1/2$ point will be deducted from the employee's point record. (If this provision is included it should be coordinated with the section on clearing the record, referenced above, so that the deduction of points corresponds with the lessening of discipline.) Employees will not accrue this $1/2$ point credit if their record is clear.

Special Review

Discipline may be accelerated in cases where there is a pattern of abuse such as but not limited to: frequent absences on Friday, Monday, or the day before or after a holiday, and instances when the employee approaches the point level for discharge, improves his attendance for a time, and then resumes a pattern of excessive absences.

Discipline may be repeated or delayed when there appear to be mitigating factors associated with the attendance problems that warrant more lenient treatment.

Sample Harassment and Sexual Harassment Policy

The following is a sample harassment and sexual harassment policy that you can distribute to your employees.

* * *

It is the policy of _____ [insert name of company] that sexual harassment or harassment of any kind of employees or applicants for employment in any form is unacceptable conduct and will not be tolerated. Harassment because of sex, race, color, age, disability, or other unlawful reasons is strictly forbidden. Employees are reminded that respect and civil behavior toward fellow employees, subordinates, and managers is expected at all times. Ridicule, making jokes at the expense of others, and other forms of harassment constitute a violation of this policy even if not unlawful.

Sexual harassment includes unwelcome sexual advances, requests for sexual favors, and other verbal, visual, or physical conduct of a sexual nature. No manager or other employee shall engage in conduct deemed to be sexual harassment, nor state or even imply that one's refusal to submit to such conduct will adversely affect that person's employment, work status, evaluation, wages, advancement, assigned duties, shifts, or any other condition of employment or career development. Similarly, no employee shall promise, imply, or grant any preferential treatment in connection with another employee or applicant engaging in sexual conduct.

The company policy is as follows:

1. It is illegal and against the policies of this company for any employee, male or female, to sexually harass any employee by:

- Making unwelcome sexual advances or requests for sexual favors, or other verbal or physical conduct of a sexual nature, a condition of an employee's continued employment

- Making submission to, or rejection of, such conduct the basis for employment decisions affecting the employee

- Creating an intimidating, hostile, or offensive working environment by such conduct

2. Any employee who feels that he or she is a victim of sexual harassment, including but not limited to that conduct listed above, by a supervisor, manager, officer, director, "owner's representative," or any other person, including fellow employees, in connection with employment with _____ [insert name of company], shall bring the matter to the *immediate* attention of the manager in charge of the location/department at which he or she is employed. An employee who is uncomfortable for any reason in bringing such a matter to the attention of this individual, or who is not satisfied that bringing the matter to the attention of such person will resolve or has resolved the matter, shall report the matter to the Human Resources or Law Department in person or by letter. Any questions about this

policy or potential sexual harassment should also be brought to the attention of the same persons. The company will promptly investigate all allegations of sexual harassment in as confidential a manner as possible and take appropriate corrective action if and where warranted. Some examples of possible appropriate corrective action include counseling, training, transfer, suspension with counseling, and/or termination of employment. Any form of retaliation against any individual for filing a bona fide complaint under this policy or for assisting in a complaint investigation is expressly prohibited.

Index